NATURE
OF THE
BRECON BEACONS

A BEGINNER'S GUIDE TO THE UPLAND ENVIRONMENT

KEVIN WALKER

Published in Great Britain 2019 by Pesda Press

Tan y Coed Canol

Ceunant

Caernarfon

Gwynedd

LL55 4RN

ISBN: 9781906095659

Printed and bound in Poland, www.hussarbooks.pl

CONTENTS

INTRODUCTION

Few people who have wandered through the hills of the Brecon Beacons National Park (BBNP) can fail to have been stirred by their surroundings … not just the shape of the land, but the rocks, plants and animals. Some are familiar – such as buttercups and blackbirds – but there are numerous others that lie unrecognised or overlooked, and plenty of facts about the familiar that are unfamiliar. This book is about those unfamiliar facts and less well-known common items; it is my attempt to bring the landscape to life.

This book will not tell you everything you need to know; it isn't supposed to be an all-encompassing guide. Far from it. It's more concerned with those everyday objects that often go unremarked – such as the familiar yellow flower that you see everywhere but cannot easily identify. Indeed, any attempt at a reasonably portable, comprehensive guide is doomed to failure from the start, simply because there is just so much to see. My difficulty has been not so much what to include (I was spoilt for choice), as what to leave out! What I have tried to do is gather together information about the more common things – the ones you are most likely to see while wandering across these delightful hills – and in doing so I've relied heavily on my own experiences of guiding and instructing throughout the area over the past four decades. Because it's a personal list, there will inevitably be things you come across that are not included – indeed, I may well have missed your personal favourites – but I make no apology for any omission as that is in the nature of the book. So, don't throw away your detailed comprehensive manuals on birds and flowers, because you will need them to identify the more obscure species … and if you do see something that I haven't mentioned, please indulge your curiosity and refer to one of the books or websites listed in the 'Further information' section at the back of this book, for it's only through knowledge that we can understand, and only through understanding that we can truly appreciate.

The Brecon Beacons National Park is a wonderful area in which to walk; full of contrasting scenery and hidden delights. Tough or gentle, it makes no difference – there is something here for everyone.

I wish you happy and inspirational walking, with clear skies and wide views.
Kevin Walker, Llangattock, 2018.

Note: Although I've used common names throughout the book, where possible I have also included the scientific (Latin) name (*in green italics*) and the Welsh name (*in red*). However, it has not been possible to find an accurate Welsh name for every species, and this is particularly true of mosses, lichens and fungi.

ACKNOWLEDGEMENTS

This book could not have been written without the help of many people, several of whom are recognised experts in their fields. In particular (and in no particular order) I must acknowledge the help, advice and encouragement given by Alan Bowring (BBNP Geopark Officer) – his vast knowledge and boundless enthusiasm for the landscape and geology of the area is an inspiration to us all, and Nicola Davies (BBNP Ecologist), who pointed me in the right direction to get specialist advice on plants and animals. Sam Bosanquet gave me valuable information and insights about mosses, liverworts and lichens, and Graham Motley helped me choose the most appropriate flowering plants. Andrew King was a mine of useful information about birds and butterflies, Norman Lowe pointed me in the right direction for moths and caterpillars, and Keith Noble helped me select the right dragonflies. These people also helped me ensure I had identified the correct species in my photographs.

Three personal friends (all Mountain Leaders) have given immense help and encouragement. Paul Williams (http://bit.ly/PaulWilliamsBirds), who runs brilliant bird walks, advised on my choice of upland birds; Julie Bell (https://simplystrolling.com), whose walks always seem to have an element of foraging, opened my eyes to the vast range of plants and fungi in the area; and Sarah Maliphant (http://more-to.org) offered good advice and relaxed walking in the Black Mountains.

Several people, including all those mentioned above, provided photographs, and these are credited individually throughout the book. All the pictures of birds were provided by Steve Wilce (https://www.breconbeaconsbirder.com).

The Pesda team have, as ever, been brilliant. Many thanks to Franco for his comments and suggestions, to Ros for proof-reading, and to Vicky for the superb layout. I would also like to thank Professor David Thorne and Dr Rhian Parry of The Welsh Place-Name Society for their help and advice in the Welsh place-names section in the final chapter.

I must also mention the book 'Nature of Snowdonia' by Mike Raine (Pesda, 2010), which in many ways was the inspiration for this volume.

It would also be remiss not to acknowledge the unwitting contribution of the hundreds of clients who, over the years, have asked searching questions about the environment through which we walk, arousing my innate curiosity and making me research the things we see and often take for granted. I have learned much from them. If, God forbid, something happened that prevented me from visiting the hills, what I would miss the most is not the physicality of walking, the adrenaline of climbing or the majesty and joy of the wide views – what I would miss the most is the camaraderie … the shared experience with like-minded souls.

Last, but by no means least, I must mention Tina, who provided encouragement, copious hot drinks and supper, and put up with my increasing irritability as the deadline approached.

To all those people I have mentioned – my grateful thanks. To any I have neglected, my humble apologies.

ROCKS

Were it not for the rocks there would be no landscape, and there is an important relationship between the hard geology and the soft environment. In the most basic terms, the birds and animals eat the plants that grow in the soil that is derived from the rocks – so it is helpful to have a rudimentary understanding of the processes that formed the ground across which we now walk.

The Central Beacons.

Waterfall country.

SETTING THE SCENE

How does one introduce the Brecon Beacons National Park in a few sentences? It is not an easy task. At first glance, the region comprises boggy upland moorland and little else, yet despite what many first-time visitors may think, there is a huge variety of scenery and habitat in this place. Admittedly, there are vast tracts of moorland with little more than the occasional enigmatic standing stone, but there are also imposing escarpments culminating in the highest mountains in southern Britain; expanses of limestone containing some of the most extensive cave systems in the UK; and deep gorges cloaked in ancient woodland, echoing to the sound of rushing torrents.

Until recently the Brecon Beacons National Park was the poor cousin of the Welsh National Parks, being less well-known and thus getting far fewer visitors than Snowdonia and the Pembrokeshire Coast. This is now changing, and year-on-year figures show that the area is rapidly growing in popularity. Despite this, it is still possible to find peace and solitude here … although you may have to wander away from the honey-pots!

Covering just over 1,350km^2 (about 520 square miles), the Park is a sizeable area, two thirds of which is built from Old Red Sandstone (ORS for short) rocks of Devonian age. Between about 420 and 360 million years old, these rocks form four distinct upland blocks, separated from each other by large river valleys.

The Black Mountains.

In the east of the Park, forming the boundary between Wales and England, lie the wide, rounded ridges of the Black Mountains, the highest point being Waun Fach (811m).

Dominating the skyline to the south of Brecon lies the magnificent escarpment of the Central Beacons. These popular peaks rise to the highest point in southern Britain at Pen y Fan (886m).

Slightly further west lies Fforest Fawr (the Great Forest) – once the hunting ground of the Tudor kings. There are several quiet hills here, the highest being Fan Fawr (734m). Water draining southwards from this region has carved the spectacular gorges of the aptly named Waterfall Country.

The most westerly block of hills is Y Mynydd Du, which confusingly translates as the Black Mountain (singular) – not to be confused with the Black Mountains (plural). To avoid confusion, many locals call this wild area the Carmarthen Fans. The highest point is Fan Brycheiniog (802m).

The ORS rocks dip gently towards the south and eventually disappear beneath younger Carboniferous rocks, comprising mainly limestones and gritstones, between about 360 and 320 million years old. These produce a dramatically different landscape characterised by limestone escarpments and pavements, bare rock and boulders, and boggy gritstone moorlands pockmarked with shakeholes. The limestone also contains some of the longest cave systems in Britain.

Along the extreme southern edge of the National Park, this sequence of rocks is hidden beneath the once economically important Coal Measures of the South Wales Coal Basin.

This basic geological sequence is interrupted by several major fault lines, and the area has also been folded and buckled by the movement of continental plates. Additionally, along the north-western boundary of the Park, there is a large geological structure – the Towy anticline – which introduces the siltstones, mudstones and grits of the older Silurian and Ordovician periods into the picture.

There are two broad groups of geological faults within the National Park. One group comprises a swarm running roughly NNW-SSE in which the rocks to the west have moved downwards relative to those on the east. The second group runs roughly NE-SW and is associated with three large 'disturbances' – zones of faults and folds extending for a considerable distance (these are the Neath, Swansea Valley and Carreg Cennen disturbances).

The Neath Disturbance runs northeast from Swansea Bay along the Vale of Neath, under Pontsticill Reservoir, across the northern edge of Mynydd Llangynidr to the valley to the north of Sugar Loaf, and on towards Hereford. The Swansea Valley Disturbance is slightly further north, also extending northeast from Swansea Bay, but heading up the Tawe Valley past Cribarth, then south of Fan Gyhirych and on past Brecon.

The Carmarthen Fans.

The Carreg Cennen Disturbance (part of the Welsh Borderland Fault Zone) is further north again, running past Llangadog and Carreg Cennen Castle, and across to the north of Sennybridge.

All are 'Caledonic' structures associated with the Caledonian Orogeny – a period of mountain building which took place between the Ordovician period and the Devonian period, between about 440 and 420 million years ago. The landscape we see today is a result not only of the geology, but also of surface processes such as glaciation and more recent river erosion. There are several major river groups here, including the Honddu, Grwyne Fawr, Grwyne Fechan and the Usk; the Taf Fawr and Taf Fechan; the Hepste, Mellte, and Nedd Fechan; and the Tawe, Twrch and Sawdde. It is these river groups that have carved the rocks into the four main areas described earlier, and formed the many V-shaped valleys that occur across the region. There are also superficial deposits. For example, there are regions of Quaternary age deposits (less than 2.6 million years old) covering much of the bedrock in the south of the Park. In the valleys, these deposits comprise clay, silt, sand and gravel, while across parts of the uplands there is a layer of glacial till. There is less superficial material in the north of the Park: mainly alluvium in the valleys and peat on parts of the sandstone uplands. The underlying rocks have a marked effect on the soil chemistry and thus on the flora and fauna. For example, limestone produces basic or alkaline soils, resulting in plants like wild thyme and green spleenwort, whereas the local gritstone produces acidic soils, resulting in plants such as sphagnum, sedge and crowberry. The ORS generally produces neutral soils, resulting in plants like harebell and tormentil.

Fforest Fawr.

Limestone area.

It is largely due to the varied sedimentary geology that the Park contains such a wealth of wildlife and so many important upland and lowland habitats. Biodiversity is extremely important here. However, it is important to remember that this is also a man-made landscape, and that every part of the environment has been affected by human activity over millennia. Ironically people often tell me how lucky I am to live in such an unspoilt area, yet the hand of man is to be seen everywhere here – from woodland clearances and coppicing, to quarrying and the production of lime. Indeed, the southern boundary of the Park is arguably the birthplace of the Industrial Revolution, as demonstrated by the ironworks at Blaenavon – a UNESCO World Heritage Site. However the main activity here has been (and still is) farming, particularly livestock farming, not just in the valleys but also on the open hillside. Indeed, the landscape we see today is largely the result of long-term grazing, where previous habitats such as woodland or dwarf shrub heath have been grazed out. There are currently about 1,000,000 sheep in the Park. When compared to the human population, that's about 30 sheep per local resident.

Tourism is of growing importance for the local economy, and walking is very popular, the main footfall being concentrated in the Central Beacons (particularly the high point of Pen y Fan, which is busy most weekends) and the Waterfall Country to the south. A well-established walking festival is held at the beginning of March each year in Crickhowell, a bustling small town centred around what is said to be the last fully independent High Street in Wales, and as a result of its success, other walking festivals now take place at Hay on Wye and Talgarth … and Llandovery has a sheep festival!

Sheep.

Pink soil.

North-east face of Pen y Fan.

A QUICK GUIDE TO THE SEDIMENTARY ROCKS

The land within the Brecon Beacons National Park is formed exclusively from sedimentary rocks, the vast majority of which started life as horizontal layers of sediment that have coalesced and hardened over time into the solid rock we see today. The sediments themselves were formed from the weathering of older rocks (as in sandstone), or from the remains of small marine animals and corals (as in limestone).

With the exception of some older Ordovician and Silurian rocks that occur in a narrow band along the north-western boundary of the area, the landscape of the Brecon Beacons National Park is formed from sedimentary rocks of the Devonian and Carboniferous periods. These rocks are formed from sand, pebbles, clay, and the remains of millions of tiny marine creatures deposited over tens of millions of years under different climatic conditions, usually under the sea, but sometimes on land.

The Devonian rocks, collectively known as the Old Red Sandstone, are largely mudstones, siltstones and sandstones, the earliest of which were laid down in desert conditions over 400 million years ago, when the land that was later to form the British Isles was located south of the equator.

This is the rock that is responsible for the area's characteristic pink-red soil. The lowest of these rocks, the Freshwater West Formation (formerly the St Maughan's Formation), are predominantly fine-grained mudstones with a few sandstone layers, which coarsen upwards into the sandstones that form the bulk of the local mountains. These are up to 850 metres thick, although this depth is not obvious as, being relatively soft, they tend to have been eroded into the lower areas.

Above the Freshwater West Formation lie the Senni Beds, which merge into the Brownstones, giving a significant layer of rocks comprising bands of hard, reddish-brown sandstones alternating with softer mudstones and siltstones. These rocks are up to 650 metres thick and can be easily seen in the precipitous north-east face of Pen y Fan and along the escarpment of the Carmarthen Fans above Llyn y Fan Fach, where thousands of years of weathering have resulted in the different strata being eroded at different rates to give a layered appearance. These rocks were laid down on a semi-arid coastal plain which was regularly inundated by seasonally flooding rivers, and it is these alternating layers of more- or less-resistant rocks that give rise to the characteristic stepped landscape which is particularly obvious in the Black Mountains.

In the middle of the Devonian Period the land rose and some of the rocks were eroded before the land sank again. Because this erosion caused some of the earlier rocks to be worn away, there is said to be an "unconformity" between the top of the Brownstones and the base of the next layer of

The stepped landscape of the Black Mountains.

Unconformity at Picws Du.

rocks – the Plateau Beds. This unconformity is obvious along the cliffs of Picws Du in the Carmarthen Fans … if you know what you are looking for! The Plateau Beds comprise thin layers of sandstones and much harder 'conglomerates' formed from a mixture of sand and pebbles. Although less than 20 metres thick, it is these beds that are responsible for the sharp edges and flat-topped summits both in the Central Beacons and further west. These rocks were laid down about 370 million years ago as the land subsided once again and the area became a coastal environment. Proof of this environment is visible in a number of places, most notably on the summit plateau of Pen y Fan, where there are extensive ripple marks

Ripple marks on summit of Pen y Fan.

Limestone at Llangattock.

in the bedrock – effectively a fossilised sandflat. One further very thin layer of rocks, the Grey Grits, occur above the Plateau Beds in a few places, particularly in the Waterfall Country in the south of the Park, and at Bryniau Gleision, to the south-west of Talybont Reservoir.

Some 359 million years ago the Devonian Period was succeeded by the Carboniferous Period. At this time, Britain lay near the equator, and the area which now forms the Brecon Beacons lay submerged under a warm, shallow tropical sea – perfect conditions for the formation of limestone which is composed of corals and the shells and exoskeletons of dead sea creatures. This rock gives a totally different landscape to that of the Old Red Sandstone – one that is characterised by outcrops of bare rock and steep, grey crags. This occurs all along the southern boundary of the Park, most spectacularly at Llangattock where it forms a long escarpment, and alongside the main A470 just north of Merthyr Tydfil. Limestone is unusual in that it is slightly soluble in rain-water, and over millions of years the cracks and joints have been dissolved away – a process that will have been going on since the limestone emerged at or near the surface. Where more-or-less horizontal layers of rock are exposed, limestone pavements have formed, a process taking tens to hundreds of thousands of years. The rock has also been dissolved away underground, and hidden from sight below the surface are some of the finest cave systems in Britain.

Gritstone moorland.

Later in the Carboniferous period, about 320 million years ago, the area became shallower again resulting in coastal swamps in which were formed soft mudstones and harder sandstones, including a series of strata known as the Marros Group, although they are commonly referred to using their former name – Millstone Grit. This series of rocks results in the boggy moorland to the south of the four main mountain areas, and it is also responsible for the famous Waterfall Country around Ystradfellte and Pontneddfechan. Eventually, the swamps became home to tropical forests

Waterfall country.

of huge horsetail plants and giant ferns, and as these died and decayed, their remains were trapped between the layers of sediment where they slowly turned into coal.

Since these rocks were deposited, Britain has moved north from the equator to its present position, and one of the results of this movement is that the rocks have been tilted so they are no longer horizontal. In broad terms, the rocks now slope down (or 'dip') towards the south by a few degrees, the Devonian and Carboniferous strata eventually disappearing under the more recent rocks of the South Wales Coal Basin. It's this tilt that causes the characteristic profile of the area – steep north-facing scarps with more gentle dip slopes to the south. The rock strata have also been compressed by the movement of the continental plates, and this has resulted in some of the rock layers becoming folded, such as can be seen on Cribarth. In some places, this compression has been more intense, resulting in some of the strata buckling into tightly folded arches such as at Bwa Maen near Pontneddfechan, or even 'snapping' along fault lines (see previous section).

Scarp and dip slope profile.

Folding – Bwa Maen.

Fault line – Hendre Quarry.

Siltstone.

Sandstones on Pen y Fan.

COMMON ROCK TYPES

In basic terms, there are four broad rock types occurring within the National Park: mudstones, sandstones, limestones, and conglomerates. In detail, the picture is slightly more complex. For example, within the mudstones and sandstones there are also siltstones and grits, some of which can be further distinguished as quartzite, ironstone, and tilestones. Within the limestone are various sub-divisions such as shelly limestone and oolitic limestone, as well as shales, rotten-stone, tufa and flowstone.

Many of these rocks contain fossils, as outlined at the end of this section.

Mudstone / *Carreg laid*

Mudstone is a very fine-grained rock comprising tiny particles of clay with a diameter of less than 0.05mm. The individual particles are so small that they are not distinguishable by the naked eye. The material that forms the mudstone was laid down in relatively calm marine environments such as tidal flats, lakes, and the deep sea. If the material is then buried beneath large quantities of other sediments, it may be heavily compressed into layers which break easily into thin flakes. If this happens the resulting 'flaky' rock is known as shale (see also below).

Siltstone / *Carreg silt*

Siltstone is a soft rock made from fine to medium-grained particles, which are intermediate in size between mudstone and sandstone. Usually pale grey or brown in colour, it is sometimes interspersed by thin layers of darker or lighter material, and it often contains ripple marks and layering – evidence of a slightly more dynamic environment than that in which mudstone is formed, but not as dynamic as that in which sandstone is formed. Although most people can distinguish individual grains of silt without magnification, particularly if they are on a contrasting background, few people can sense them when rolled between their fingers. Some experienced geologists and soil scientists detect silt particles by gently biting them between their front teeth … but this is not recommended!

Sandstone / *Tywodfaen*

Sandstone is made from particles of between 0.05mm and 2mm in diameter, which may have been deposited in the sea, in rivers or in deserts. The loose material is then cemented together by minerals precipitated from ground-water. Most sandstones contain a large proportion of quartz grains simply because quartz is a very hard, chemically-resistant mineral. However, many sandstones also contain grains of other minerals like calcite, clay, or mica.

Gritstone / *Carreg grut*

Gritstone (or sometimes simply 'grit') is a hard, coarse-grained sandstone, often containing angular sand grains, and sometimes even small pebbles. It often sparkles in the sun because the light reflects off the faces of quartz crystals, and it feels coarse to the touch – a bit like stroking sandpaper! The term 'Millstone Grit' was applied in northern England to a type of grit extensively quarried for millstones used to mill flour, to grind wood into pulp for paper-making, and for grindstones to sharpen blades. This practice was not so common in Wales, although millstone quarries did exist here.

Far from being a dead science, geology is alive and kicking, and new discoveries are being made on a regular basis. As a result of some of these advances in knowledge, the term 'Millstone Grit' has fallen out of favour with geologists in south Wales, who have replaced it with the term 'Marros Group'.

Conglomerate / *Amryfaen*

Conglomerates are made from coarse, rounded particles of greater than 2mm in diameter, cemented together by smaller particles or by minerals precipitated from groundwater after the sediment was deposited. Particles of this size can only be moved by strong currents, so the original sediments must have been deposited in a dynamic environment such as that found along fast-flowing rivers or beaches with strong waves or tides. Additionally, the rounded shape of the individual particles indicates that they were tumbled by moving waves or water, which further suggests that there must have been a good source of large particles somewhere up-current. The most commonly found conglomerates within the Park – those within the Twrch Sandstones – contain pebbles (or 'clasts') composed almost entirely of quartz.

Many conglomerates begin life as layers of pebbles or cobbles. The finer material – sand and clay – is then deposited on top, and slowly works its way down through the layer to fill in the gaps. Finally, the minerals precipitated from the ground-water act as a cement and bind everything together. If the main cementing mineral is calcareous, the rock is known as 'calcrete'.

Gritstone.

Examples of conglomerate (and right).

Quartzite / *Cwartsit*

Quartzite is the name given to very hard, quartz-rich sandstones and grit-stones that may comprise over 97% silica. The purest quartzites in the area occur within the Twrch Sandstone formation (once known as the Basal Grit), which occurs across southern parts of the Park, particularly at Craig y Ddinas (Dinas Rock) and in the nearby Nedd Fechan gorge. These rocks were mined and quarried from the late 18th century until as recently as 1964, the material being ground into a fine sand which was then used to make firebricks to line the insides of blast-furnaces. These bricks were of such high quality that they were exported world-wide ... indeed, the Russian for "firebrick" is "dinas"!

Silica sand was also extracted from shattered Twrch Sandstone at Penwyllt and on Cribarth (both in the upper Swansea Valley), and from various locations in the west of the Park such as between Foel Fraith and Cefn Carn Fadog, and near Herbert's Quarry at the top of the A4069 between Brynaman and Llangadog.

Tilestone / *Teilfaen*

From a geologist's viewpoint, the Tilestones Formation is a band of mica-rich sandstone dating from the Upper Silurian period but marking the lowermost part of the ORS. The high mica content of this rock means that it can be split readily into thin sheets suitable for use as roofing tiles. These rocks outcrop on Mynydd Myddfai in the west of the Park, and old tilestone quarries – sometimes mistaken as the remains of ditch and rampart forti-fications – can be traced right along the ridge. Such was the importance and success of these tilestone quarries that people looked for similar rocks elsewhere, finding plenty of opportunity within the Brownstones and Senni Beds of the ORS ... although nowhere were they as good as those found within the Silurian Tilestones Formation. Often these alternative sites were quarried to produce thicker slabs suitable for use as work surfaces and flooring. The thickest slabs were used as building stone.

Silica mine entrance.

Tilestone quarry.

Ironstone / *Haearnfaen*

Ironstone is a fine-grained sedimentary deposit which contains a sufficiently large amount of iron compounds that it can be smelted commercially. The iron itself originally came either from iron rich soils, or from deposits in which the iron content was unusually high due to chemical processes caused by organic matter. It is particularly common along the southern borders of the Park where it runs alongside the South Wales Coalfield. Indeed, the Welsh iron industry owed its existence to the presence of good quality ironstone, limestone and coal in the same area.

Farewell Rock / *Y Garreg Ddiffaith*

No discussion of local rocks would be complete without at least a passing mention of Farewell Rock. Comprising a narrow sequence of sandstones, this occurs widely across the base of the Lower Coal Measures in the South Wales Coalfield, and was originally named by the ironstone miners who knew that, once reached, they could say farewell to any more ironstone as there was none beneath it. Eventually the term was adopted by the coal miners for the same reason – there are no coal seams below the Farewell Rock.

Limestone / *Calchfaen*

Limestone is different from other rocks in two respects: first, it's composed mainly of crushed organic remains such as corals, shells and skeletons (which means it contains many fossils); secondly, it's soluble in rain water! The rocks contain two minerals – calcite and aragonite – both of which are crystalline forms of calcium carbonate, and it is these minerals which cause the rock to dissolve in slightly acidic water (see the section Caves and cave formation). Indeed, if you pour vinegar or any form of acid onto limestone rocks, they will slowly bubble and fizz – the stronger the acid, the more violent the reaction.

There are several different forms of limestone varying in colour from white, through varying shades of grey, to black. These rocks make up about 10% of all sedimentary rocks and have been exploited commercially for hundreds (if not thousands) of years – first for building materials, then for lime, and more recently as a flux in the smelting of iron and other metals, and for cement. Most of the quarries along the southern boundary of the Park are limestone quarries.

Shale / *Siâl*

Shale is a type of laminar mudstone made from clay-sized particles that are too small to see with the naked eye. The main difference between mudstone and shale is that mudstone breaks into blocks, whereas shale breaks into thin plates or chips with roughly parallel tops and bases ... a bit like slate.

Limestone.

Shale.

Rotten-stone / *Garreg bwdr*

Rotten-stone (a.k.a. rottenstone and Tripoli) is the product of near-surface weathering of a sandy limestone that used to be known as the Upper Limestone shale. This was once valued as an abrasive and polishing agent for use in the metalwork and woodwork industries, and was quarried from various locations in the south-west of the Park, particularly to the north-west of Cribarth where it was extensively worked in the 19th century. In basic terms, the natural erosion of the rock removed the soluble calcium carbonate and left a pumice-like material composed of fine particles of abrasive silica sand.

Tufa / *Twffa*

Tufa is a very porous variety of limestone formed by the precipitation of calcite or aragonite from supersaturated water. It is often brownish in colour due to iron oxide impurities. In many cases, biological processes involving the metabolism of algae and bacteria affect the concentration of the calcium carbonate, but in areas of limestone quarrying (such as those found along the southern boundary of the Park) spring water flowing through the waste material from limekilns becomes supersaturated with calcium carbonate, with the result that streambeds become coated with layers of tufa and pools of standing water become coated with films of cyanobacteria. In fact, anything the supersaturated water touches can become coated, so fresh tufa often contains the remains of leaves, twigs and flowers.

Tufa.

Flowstone.

Flowstone / *Carreg ddylif*

Flowstone is a sheet-like layer of limestone minerals formed where saturated water flows over walls and floors and deposits thin layers of some of the dissolved material it contains. Over time, these layers can build up and become quite thick. Although most flowstone formation occurs in caves (stalactites and stalagmites being two well-known examples), flowstone can also occur on the surface where, for example, saturated water flows in a thin sheet down a rock face. Given sufficient time, these flowstone sheets build up to form the classic 'organ-pipe' structure, good examples of which can be seen on many of the old quarried faces along the Llangattock Escarpment south of Crickhowell.

Fossils

Fossils are the remains of ancient plants and creatures that have literally been turned to stone. All sedimentary rocks can contain fossils, and the rocks which form the landscape of the Brecon Beacons National Park are no exception.

Many of the sites where fossils have been found in quantity are designated as Sites of Special Scientific Interest (SSSIs), and the use of hammers and removing fossils is strictly forbidden. However, it is possible to come across fossils virtually anywhere. For example, several old quarries along the northern boundary of the Park contain fossil ferns, and rare fossil fish have also been found. The planet's first forests came into existence during the Devonian period, and fossil leaves and even fossilised tree trunks have been found within the ORS.

The Carboniferous rocks contain fossils of crinoids, molluscs and corals – indeed, it can be argued that limestone is composed almost entirely of fossils! Some people believe that the most spectacular fossils to be seen in the National Park are Lithostrotion coral, whose intricate internal detail is often beautifully preserved. If you hanker to see fossils, a good place to start is on the geology trail from Craig y Nos Country Park to Cribarth, in the old limestone quarries that abound along the southern boundary of the Park, or around Carreg yr Ogof in the west of the Park.

Fossil shells.

Fossil shells.

Lithostrotion coral.

Lithostrotion coral.

Lithostrotion coral.

Fossilised plant stem.

Cave entrance.

ROCKS – CAVES AND CAVE FORMATION

CAVES AND CAVE FORMATION

A narrow band of Carboniferous Limestone runs across the southern part of the National Park, stretching from the Blorenge in the east to Carreg Cennen in the west. These rocks were formed around 350 million years ago in a shallow tropical sea, and nowadays form a landscape known by geomorphologists as Karst (see also below). This is characterised by steep cliffs and bare rock outcrops, caves, springs and dry valleys, limestone pavements, shakeholes and calcareous grasslands, each with their own unique and sometimes rare flora and fauna. For example, the cliffs and old quarry faces are home to several rare plants including three unique species of whitebeam, and they also provide nesting sites for birds such as ravens and peregrine falcons. In addition to these important surface features, it is in this thin belt of limestone, 75km long but rarely more than 1.5km wide, that some of the finest and most extensive cave systems in Britain occur. These once provided shelter for bears, but nowadays they are only used by bats, badgers and cavers!

Cave formation

Limestone is composed largely of calcium carbonate, which is slightly soluble in acidic water. The precise chemistry is complex, involving the alteration of calcium carbonate to calcium hydrogen carbonate and the effects of carbonic acid, but the details are way beyond the scope of this book. Suffice it to say that the rain water landing on the Brecon Beacons is already slightly acidic due to atmospheric carbon dioxide and pollutants, and this water then picks up more acidity from the peat soils on which it lands. The end result, when it flows onto the limestone, is that it starts to dissolve the rock, concentrating along lines of weakness such as cracks and joints. Over time, these cracks and joints widen into open tubes and fissures which eventually become what we know as cave passages. These run along more-or-less horizontal cracks (or bedding planes) between different layers of rock, and also along more-or-less vertical joints which formed as the rock flexed due to earth movements.

The level below which the ground is saturated with water is known as the *water table*. Passages formed below the water table are known as *phreatic*, and are often round or tubular in cross-section, because being full of water they are eroded equally on all surfaces. The water in these flooded passages can also flow uphill due to the pressure of water above! Passages formed

Bedding plane cave.

Phreatic passage.

Pot hole.

above the water table are known as *vadose* and have air in them. They often appear as rifts, because the water can only erode downwards due to gravity. Where passages become sufficiently large, roof collapse can occur, and this can have a major impact on cavern formation and development.

In the same way that the cave grows, so the surface topography evolves, and this has an effect on the cave's development. Rivers and glaciers carve valleys resulting in a lowering of the water table, and this can leave passages that were previously phreatic in the vadose zone. This results in passages with a keyhole-shaped profile – a phreatic tube in which there is a vadose rift.

Where there is air in the passage, as in the vadose zone, water that is saturated with dissolved limestone trickles down walls and through cracks in the cave roof. As this happens, the process of evaporation results in a small amount of pure calcium carbonate being left behind. Over thousands of years, this deposited material built up into cave formations such as flowstone curtains and stalactites. Where water drips from the base of a curtain or stalactite and hits solid ground, the splashing effect causes more evaporation, which in turn leads to the growth of stalagmites and more flowstone. Cavers call these decorations 'pretties', and there is an almost infinite variety, ranging from branching helictites that appear to defy gravity, through fragile straw stalactites and crystal pools, to huge flowstone curtains and stalagmite bosses.

Karst

Karst is the technical terms for a limestone landscape comprising caves, dry valleys, shakeholes and limestone pavements – a term derived from a region of the same name in Slovenia where such features predominate. However, the Brecon Beacons karst landscape is different to other such areas in the UK in that it has fewer limestone pavements (see below) but many more shakeholes. Indeed, geomorphologists from all over the world come to the Brecon Beacons National Park to study shakehole formation, a favourite study area being on Mynydd Llangynidr south-west of Crickhowell.

Shakeholes

Shakeholes look like bomb craters, and can form in one of two ways. First they can occur on limestone areas where a covering of boulder clay left after the last Ice Age is washed into cracks and fissures by surface water. Secondly they can form on gritstone moorland where the limestone is only a short distance below the surface. In this instance, the craters form either where sections of cave collapse within the limestone, resulting in depressions on the surface, or where the surface rocks collapse into solution pockets formed along the limestone / gritstone boundary. The process is exaggerated in this area because the local gritstone is heavily fractured or jointed, and therefore cannot support its own weight.

The greatest concentration of shakeholes in north-west Europe is on the gritstone moorland of Mynydd Llangynidr to the south-west of Crickhowell, as a consequence of which the area has been designated as a Site of Special Scientific Interest (SSSI). The moor is widely regarded as being one of the best examples of an interstratal karst. Many of the holes both here and on the neighbouring Mynydd Llangatwg are truly spectacular – some are more than 60m wide and over 25m deep, and several have streams flowing into them, particularly in or shortly after wet weather, the water usually disappearing underground (although some shakeholes are permanently flooded). There are also many examples of intermittent pools in the area, the water collecting in wet periods, but soon seeping underground when the rain stops, sometimes leaving an obvious 'drain-hole' in the peaty bed of the pool.

Karst landscape.

Shakeholes.

Shakeholes.

Shakeholes.

Intermittent pool.

Flooded shakehole.

Limestone pavements

During the last ice age (just over ten thousand years ago), the ice scraped away at the land and exposed parts of the thin band of limestone running along the southern boundary of the Park, often grinding it smooth. Over the succeeding millennia, the smoothed rock has been corroded by rainwater as described above, resulting in the formation of *Limestone Pavements* – flattish areas of rock characterised by blocks (known as clints) separated by cracks and fissures (known as grykes or grikes). These pavements are small and scattered, their combined total area being less than about 20 hectares, but they represent one of the scarcest habitats in Wales.

In the past, many pavements were damaged by the removal of the clints for building work or decorative stone-work; those that remain are now protected as they represent a unique habitat. The narrow, sometimes deep grykes offer plants protection against both grazing sheep and exposure to the worst of the elements, and this often results in micro-climates suitable for plants such as limestone fern and lily-of-the-valley. The flowers attract insects, which in turn attract birds and small animals, and the (sometimes) sun-drenched rocks attract slow-worms and common lizards. In the Ogof Ffynnon Ddu National Nature Reserve (NNR) near Penwyllt in the Swansea Valley, the limestone pavements are particularly noteworthy and provide a habitat for several rare plants including mossy saxifrage and autumn gentian.

Limestone pavement.

Limestone pavement with fossils in foreground. © Julie Bell.

Some areas have been fenced to prevent damage by grazing sheep.

In other areas where the pavements have not been affected by grazing, they have often become overgrown with woodland. These wooded pavements provide shelter for small mammals such as mice and voles, while the bare rock and shade provide perfect habitats for mosses and lichens.

Limestone pavement.

U-shaped valley.

V-shaped valley.

THE ICE AGE AND BEYOND

The rocks that form the Brecon Beacons National Park have been repeatedly covered by ice during a series of Ice Ages over the last two million years. This ice has carved the landscape into the shape we see today. During each ice age, snow falling onto the predominantly flat-topped mountains was blown by the prevailing south-westerly winds onto the more sheltered northern and eastern slopes where it accumulated, slowly turning to ice. Eventually these ice fields spawned small glaciers that started to flow downhill, and this movement gouged out hollows, the back-walls of which were steepened by frost-shattering, forming glacial cwms. At the height of the ice ages the many small glaciers merged into rivers of ice that carved large U-shaped valleys, resulting in the drainage system we see today. The Usk Glacier started in what is now the Carmarthen Fans, then flowed east over Brecon where it merged with more ice coming from the Central Beacons. The enlarged glacier then continued on over what is now Crickhowell before turning south towards Usk. The Towy Glacier flowed southwest over Llandovery and Llandeilo, continuing towards Carmarthen, while other major glaciers flowed towards Swansea forming the valleys of the Tawe and the Neath, and towards Cardiff forming the valley of the Taff. Each ice age effectively destroyed or at least modified the effects of the previous ice age, so it is the most recent – the Devensian Ice Age – that has left the most obvious features. This was at its height about 20,000 years ago, but although the ice sheet then dissipated over the next few thousand years, a short-lived cold snap called the Younger Dryas occurred about 12,000 years ago resulting in the formation of several small glaciers in the mountains of Snowdonia and the Brecon Beacons. Subsequent rapid warming in north-west Europe then led to the retreat of the ice and the development of a wooded landscape, remnants of which are still visible today ... but the evidence of glaciation still remains.

U-shaped and V-shaped valleys

As glaciers scour the landscape, they form valleys with a characteristic U-shaped cross section, with a flat bottom and steep, straight side walls. Rivers, on the other hand, form valleys with a characteristic V-shaped cross section and often curving side walls. Generally speaking, the steeper the angle of descent of the river, the tighter the cross-section of the V – thus the higher up the mountain, the narrower the valley.

Glacial cwms

There are many glacial cwms with frost-steepened back walls, such as can be seen all along the northern escarpment of the Central Beacons. These were largely formed by a combination of freeze-thaw action shattering the rocks, which then fell onto the snow field below. As the snow accumulated it turned into ice, which then began to move downslope as a glacier. This took the rocks with it, eventually dumping them as moraine.

Moraine

As the glaciers moved forward, they pushed rocks and soil in front of them like a bulldozer, and scraped rocks and boulders from the sides of the valleys they were forming. This material, together with the rocks that fell from above due to frost-shattering, is known as moraine. Where this lies at the end of a glacier it is known as Terminal Moraine; where it lies along the sides of the glacier it is known as Lateral Moraine; where it forms where two glaciers meet and run alongside each other it is known as Medial Moraine. Many of the higher valleys have floors which are full of lumps and bumps – evidence of the rock debris which was dumped by the glaciers as they retreated.

Moraine dammed lakes

As the climate warmed and the ice began to retreat, the glaciers left behind ridges of moraine that formed dams behind which meltwater could collect. A good example is Llyn Cwm Llwch, a Geological Conservation Review Site, widely regarded as the best preserved glacial lake in South Wales. Its waters are hemmed in by a dam of glacial moraine left by a small glacier that occupied the cwm during the Younger Dryas ice age. Other good examples of moraine dammed lakes include Llyn y Fan Fach and Llyn y Fan Fawr, both in the Carmarthen Fans.

Glacial cwm.

Moraine dammed lake.

Pro-talus rampart.

Pro-talus ramparts

Pro-talus ramparts are ridges of loose rock (now stabilised and grassed-over) running beneath and parallel to a line of cliffs. These ramparts were formed when frost-shattered rocks fell from a cliff onto the steep-angled snow fields that remained for many years after the ice had retreated, eventually sliding down the slope to accumulate at its base. When the snow and ice melted, the material remained as a long ridge. A good example of what many geomorphologists believe to be a pro-talus rampart can be seen at Fan Fechan, running below and parallel to the awesome ridge of Fan Hir in the Carmarthen Fans.

Erratics

Erratics are large chunks of rock that have been carried by glaciers away from their original location and dumped elsewhere. It is this process that explains the presence of large boulders of Old Red Sandstone in the middle of an area of Carboniferous Limestone.

Glacial striations

Glacial striations are long straight scratches on slabs of bedrock, formed by fragments of rock frozen into the base of a moving glacier. As the glacier moves, immense pressure is brought to bear on these rock fragments, which gouge the bedrock rock beneath. Geomorphologists can use glacial striations to deduce the direction in which a glacier flowed.

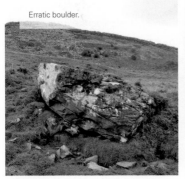

Erratic boulder.

Glacial striations.

Till

Also known as Boulder Clay, till is a mixture of small boulders, gravel, sand and clay, which comprises the material eroded by the glaciers. Its precise composition varies depending upon the rocks below the glacier. Many areas of the Park are coated in a layer of till, although in some places this is concealed below a layer of peat. This is particularly true in the Black Mountains. In other places, such as at Traeth Mawr on the common above Libanus, hollows in the till have become filled with peat, resulting in raised bogs. These are important wetland habitats with a rich wildlife, and the peat deposits provide a valuable insight into the climate of the area over the past 12,000 years.

Traeth mawr.

Peat.

Post glacial features

The period since the last Ice Age is known as the Holocene, or (in the UK at least) as the Flandrian Interglacial. Throughout this period, large amounts of till and other material have moved slowly downslope – a process known as *solifluction* – so as a general rule, the till is thicker in the base of valleys than along the sides.

Solifluction.

Streams starting high up in the mountains have carved gullies which merge into V-shaped valleys, many of which occur across the region. Several have sculpted deep, flat-based terraces through the glacial debris. As they descend into the larger valleys, these small streams merge to form major rivers such as the Usk, the Taff and the Towy, and these in turn have deposited large areas of sand and gravel sourced largely from the till further downstream, often forming wide flood-plains.

Slopes that were over-steepened by frost shattering or glacial erosion are now slowly trying to reach a more stable angle, and *Post-Glacial Landslips* have occurred throughout the region. These occur almost exclusively in the Brownstones of the ORS, and there are some remarkable examples involving huge chunks of land. The scarred profile of the Skirrid (Ysgyryd Fawr) is the result of one such landslip, and at Cwmyoy the ancient church is remarkably twisted and bent because it was built across a block of land that was still moving ... and continues to move, albeit slowly.

River terracing.

Usk flood plain.

Skirrid.

Two excellent but differing examples are obvious on the hillside above Crickhowell. The Darren, to the north-west, is a classic example of a post-glacial landslip, the slipped material looking much like quarry spoil below the cliffs. The landslip that formed Table Mountain *(Crug Hywel)*, the flat-topped hill to the north-east, is of a different type and magnitude, and is considered to be a classic example of a *block slump*, where a relatively coherent chunk of strata has detached from its original position and slid en-masse along a relatively flat surface such as the boundary between a permeable and an impermeable layer.

Smaller examples of landslips are common and are visible as rocky scars on hillsides, a good example being along the eastern slopes of Fan Frynych, south of Brecon. Additionally, mudflows still occur with surprising frequency, streaking the steeper slopes of the mountains dull pink, and these are particularly noticeable along the escarpments of the Central Beacons and the Carmarthen Fans.

These processes are still happening ... proof that geology is not just a thing of the past – it's a continuing process.

Table Mountain.

Mud slides.

PLANTS

Unlike rocks, plants are seasonal … which creates potential issues when trying to identify them! Spring and summer are good times to see them; many die away in autumn; and many are dead (or at least dormant) in winter. Those that are still visible in winter are often sad and bedraggled and look little like they do in summer, which can be confusing. For example, wimberry (page 128) is little more than a series of bare, leafless stalks, while rosettes of foxglove leaves (page 148) appear long before the flowering stems.

This is not to say that you should not look for plants in winter. Depending upon the weather, some plants can flower early in the season, the most common being purple saxifrage (page 120) and, of course, snowdrops (page 151). Additionally, the bare ground and sparsity of flowering vegetation makes winter an ideal time to spot mosses, club mosses, liverworts and lichens.

Sphagnum.

Bristly haircap (and closeup inset). © Sam Bosanquet.

MOSSES / MWSOGLAU

Mosses have been around for over 400 million years, making them one of the oldest plant groups on Earth. They have extremely varied ecological needs and can be found throughout the year in almost every habitat in the area … from tarmac pavements to the summit of Pen y fan. They are mainly green (especially in wet weather), flowerless, simple-structured plants that reproduce asexually or by producing spores, and they play an important role in ecosystems by capturing water and nutrients, mainly through their leaves. They also inhibit soil erosion, provide a place for plant seedlings to germinate, and offer shelter for micro-fauna and other tiny creatures. Squirrels use moss to line their dreys, birds sometimes use it to line their nests, and dormice hibernate in nests made beneath it.

There are almost 1,200 types of moss in Europe, about two-thirds of which grow in the British Isles. Many types look remarkably similar, making them difficult to identify; indeed common names are often different in different areas, and may even be swapped between species. To add to the confusion, one of the most common 'mosses' – reindeer moss – is actually not a moss at all, but a lichen!

Over 550 different mosses and liverworts have been recorded in the National Park. Rather than attempt to list them all, I have included a few of the more common species. If you want more information, please consult one of the specialist books mentioned in the further information section at the end of the book ... and use a magnifying glass (like the one on your compass!) to aid identification!

Sphagnum / *Migwyn*

Of the 400 species of sphagnum that occur worldwide, 36 have been recorded in the UK, and most of these are to be found in Wales. They range in colour from green and orange to red and pink. Individual plants are small, but they tend to clump together to form spongy carpets and hummocks, which eventually decay to form peat. Although they have varied ecology, they are largely restricted to wet places; some are only found on bogs, while others are in 'flushes' where water moves slowly downhill, and one species grows only on steep woodland slopes. Even when dead, sphagnum plants can hold large quantities of water inside their cells, sometimes as much as 25 times their dry weight, and this helps them retain water in drier conditions. It also makes them extremely unpleasant for walkers!

Dried sphagnum has many uses. Being absorptive and acidic, it inhibits the growth of bacteria and has been used since medieval times as a wound dressing. Native Americans use it as nappy material, and the Inuit use it for insulation. Dried peat, too, has many uses. It has been used as a fuel for millennia, is critical in the commercial growing of mushrooms, and is also used to flavour whisky and smoke fish. The very slow rates of decay found in peat bogs help preserve plant fragments and foodstuffs, and pots of butter over 2,000 years old have been recovered. Human and animal remains have also been found, but while flesh, clothing and hair have been preserved, the acidity of the peat means that the bones have often dissolved.

Bristly haircap *(Polytrichum piliferum)*

This patch-forming moss has long white hairs protruding from its leaf tip, and it sometimes has bright red rosettes of central leaves in summer. It is low-growing (usually 5cm or less) with a characteristic shape, the 3mm-long leaves being densely clustered at the shoot tip, leaving the reddish stem somewhat bare below. In summer it produces angular, 4 or 5-faced spore capsules on 1–3cm long, reddish stalks. Although very similar to juniper haircap (see below), and an effective colonist of disturbed ground, it prefers more open, mobile ground and is frequent on loose surfaces such as path edges, scree beds, shingly river banks and gravelly pond margins.

Broom forkmoss. © Sam Bosanquet.

Broom forkmoss *(Dicranum scoparium)* **Fforchfwsogl**

This common woodland moss forms dense cushions of vegetation up to 10cm thick. It has thin, tapering leaves up to 7mm long, with long, toothed tips. The spore capsules are cylindrical, and form on a long yellow stem with a reddish underside.

Common haircap *(Polytrichum commune)* *Eurwallt y forwyn*

Also known as star moss and common hair moss, this grows in large clumps in damp areas all over the hills. The stems are usually between about 10cm and 30cm long (although they can be as short as 2cm or as long as 70cm), and they have 8–12mm long narrow pointed leaves that curve away from the stem, giving a starry appearance viewed from above. In dry conditions, these twist gently around the stems. In summer, 4-sided box-like spore capsules rise up to 12cm above the leaves on red stalks. Tea made from common haircap was once believed to dissolve kidney stones and was also used as a rinse to strengthen and beautify women's hair. The stems have been used to make brooms and brushes, and have been woven or plaited to make mats, rugs, baskets, and cloaks.

Common tamarisk moss *(Thuidium tamariscinum)* *Pluen-fwsogl y coed*

The bright yellow-green fern-like shoots make this one of our more distinctive mosses. The green or brown stems are covered with tiny hairs and broad, heart-shaped leaves about 1.25mm long. It forms loose mats, 5cm to 25cm across, and grows on soil in woodland, in hedge banks and damp, grassy places.

Cypress-leaved plait-moss *(Hypnum cupressiforme)* *Pluen-fwsogl cypreswydd*

This common moss has irregularly branched, slender shoots about 2cm long, with tiny, curved leaves that taper to a long point. It has low, creeping stems which form dense mats, and typically grows on tree trunks, logs, and walls. It was formerly used as a filling for pillows and mattresses.

Frizzled crisp-moss *(Tortella tortuosa)*

A curly-leaved moss, this forms yellow-green cushions several centimetres deep in limestone areas. When moist, the 7mm long narrow leaves have wavy margins; when dry, these shrivel into a tangle of contorted spirals. Small tufts can be found on limestone boulders, walls, scree or pavements, and larger patches form on cliffs.

Common haircap

Common tamarisk moss. © Graham Motley

Cypress-leaved plait-moss. © Sam Bosanquet.

Frizzled crisp-moss. © Sam Bosanquet.

Golden-head moss *(Breutelia chrysocoma)*

This attractive species forms loose, furry patches or grows as scattered, yellowish shoots flecked with red and gold. Each shoot is usually less than 10cm tall, but occasionally more. It has widely spreading, narrowly triangular leaves between 2.5–4mm long, and a red stem, the base of which is sheathed with a brown felt giving it the appearance of a bottle-brush. Although it prefers open, unshaded, acidic ground such as bog, heathland and damp rock ledges, it can also be found on limestone pavements and in woodland.

Greater fork-moss *(Dicranum majus)* Fforch-fwsogl

You will find this large moss forming extensive patches, particularly in the Waterfall Country to the south of Fforest Fawr. The 15mm leaves are uniformly curved, giving them the appearance of scimitars. It prefers sheltered, acidic ground, and will only grow on rock if there is a build-up of organic material.

Grey-cushioned grimmia *(Grimmia pulvinata)* Clustog arian

This moss forms round, almost furry, grey cushions about 1–2cm tall on dry rocks and walls. The narrow, 3–4mm leaves have a long white hair-like point that reflects sunlight and helps prevent the moss from drying out. In moist conditions, the cushions can appear dark green; when dry, the leaves contract and the silvery points curl together, making them particularly noticeable.

Juniper haircap *(Polytrichum juniperinum)*

Although sometimes found where there is moisture, juniper haircap more usually grows in dry, acidic, exposed habitats. It has reddish stems and grey-green leaves with a distinctive red-brown tip – a characteristic which distinguishes it from bristly haircap. Between 1cm and 7cm tall, it is an early coloniser of areas that have been disturbed by heath fires or clearfelling, and it is a strong stabilising plant – a colony of haircap can hold a vertical 20cm bank of gravel in place. Herbalists considered juniper haircap a powerful diuretic, and a tea made from this moss was used to treat urinary obstructions and oedema. Because it caused no nausea, it was considered an excellent remedy when it was necessary to continue treatment indefinitely.

Golden-head moss. © Sam Bosanquet.

Greater fork-moss. © Sam Bosanquet.

Grey-cushioned grimmia.

Juniper haircap. © Sam Bosanquet.

Little shaggy-moss. © Sam Bosanquet.
Mountain fern moss. © Graham Motley.

Little shaggy-moss *(Rhytidiadelphus loreus)*

This spreading moss has a red stem and 15–20cm long shoots, with small (3mm) pointed leaves which all point more or less in the same direction. It likes acidic woods in upland districts, and is common in the Waterfall Country to the south of Fforest Fawr. It also occurs in acidic grassland and on heathery slopes in the mountains.

Mountain fern moss *(Hylocomium splendens) Mwsogl rhedyn mynydd*

This common moss is known by various names including splendid feather moss, glittering wood moss, and stairstep moss – so-called because it sometimes has a stepped appearance due to varying growth rates during successive seasons. Although similar to common tamarisk moss, it can be distinguished as it has red stems and broader leaves. It is often abundant among grass and heather on heaths and moorlands, and also grows in coniferous woodlands.

Smaller white-moss *(Leucobryum juniperoideum) Mwsogl gwyn llai*

Found in both deciduous and coniferous woodlands, this whitish-green moss forms flat patches which grow to become domed and eventually evolve into rounded cushions up to 30cm across. It grows on acidic soil and rock edges, and favours well-rotted wood in moderate shade.

Smaller white-moss. © Sam Bosanquet.

Springy turf-moss *(Rhytidiadelphus squarrosus)*

This common moss forms dense mats in grassland, and sometimes in heath and wetlands. The shoots, which can grow to 15cm long, are at right angles to the base, and spread out in all directions, giving the plant a star-like appearance. The stems are red, but are often completed cloaked by the leaves. The usually rare, bud-like spore capsules are relatively frequent in some areas of the Park.

Woolly fringe-moss *(Racomitrium lanuginosum)* **Mwsogl gwlanog**

Also known as hoary rock-moss, this common upland moss often forms downy carpets in rocky areas. It has very curly white hairs at the ends of its shoots giving it a distinctive grey appearance. In addition to windswept ridges and dry scree, it also grows on the tops of drystone walls, in dry turf, and in bogs.

Springy turf-moss. © Sam Bosanquet.

Woolly fringe-moss.

Dripwort. © Sam Bosanquet.

Water earwort. © Sam Bosanquet.

LIVERWORTS / LLYSIAU'R AFU

Liverworts are very simple plants. Worldwide, there are almost 9,000 species, and while they are not economically important to humans, they provide food for animals and aid the decay of wood and the disintegration of rocks. You will only find them in wet places, so one of the best places to find them is in the Waterfall Country to the south of Fforest Fawr, where rushing torrents throw spray into the air and the dense tree canopy prevents the moisture from evaporating.

There are almost 300 species of liverworts in the UK, divided into two broad types: *Thallose liverworts* have a plate-like body (the thallus) and no leaves; *Leafy liverworts* have two ranks of flattened leaves growing from a stem, with a third rank of smaller, forked leaves underneath. Identifying different species is extremely difficult and requires specialist knowledge, but I have included details of four of the more common.

Dripwort *(Pellia epiphylla)* **Llysiau'r afu llyfn**

As its name suggests, dripwort likes to grow on surfaces that are always dripping wet, but not standing in water. It loves shade, and tends to favour banks and rock faces under ledges, where it can mass together in huge patches several metres wide. It has smooth, flat, fleshy leaves, which grow up to a centimetre across. These are irregular in shape and dull-green in colour, with wavy paler edges.

Water earwort *(Scapania undulata)*

This liverwort has amazing, rounded two-lobed leaves (1–3mm long), each lobe growing face-to-face with its neighbour. It often grows in large spongy mounds with shoots several centimetres long. It is quite variable, and although it is most commonly dark green, it can be reddish, yellowish or even bright purple! It loves very wet places, and prefers to grow on rocks in streams and flushes, or around upland springheads.

Greater featherwort *(Plagiochila asplenioides)* **Llysiau'r afu plethog**

This translucent-leaved beauty is large and distinctive, with strong stems up to 12cm long and 1cm wide, and neat rows of bright or pale green, crinkly rounded leaves along each side. The leaves are angled towards the tip of the stem and overlap each other. It grows in a wide range of habitats, from damp turf in sheltered woodland and more open places, to rocks and rotting wood, and along stream banks and hedgerows.

Greater whipwort *(Bazzania trilobata)*

Also known as three-lobed liverwort, this is one of the most distinctive liverworts of ancient oak woodlands, and is particularly eye-catching in western parts of the National Park where it grows in bright green or brownish-green mounds, up to 10cm across. It has 4–6mm-wide shoots with rounded backs, and tiny, downward-pointing 2.5mm-wide leaves. Most common on the ground and on rocks, it can also be found on tree trunks and logs, and is seldom found away from woodland.

Greater featherwort. © Sam Bosanquet.

Greater whipwort. © Sam Bosanquet.

Great scented liverwort. © Sam Bosanquet.

Great scented liverwort *(Conocephalum conicum) Llysiau'r afu llydanddail*

Also known as snakeskin liverwort, this forms large, dark green mats. The heavily scented thalli are up to 17mm wide, flat and smooth with a leathery surface, sometimes with purple edges. As the plant matures, it begins to resemble snakeskin, developing a hexagonal pattern on the surface, with conspicuous air pores within the hexagons.

Fir club moss.

CLUB MOSSES / CNWPFWSOGLAU

During the late Carboniferous period, some 350 million years ago, club mosses were one of the most dominant plant species, covering much of what is now the southern part of the Brecon Beacons National Park in a dense forest. Along with horsetails, they could grow to over 30 metres tall, and it is their remains that formed the coal of the South Wales coalfield. By comparison, modern club mosses are tiny!

Nowadays there are three species of club moss in the Park ... although they are actually quite difficult to find, and one is really rare. They are considered to be more evolved than mosses because they have specialised fluid-conducting tissues, which mosses lack. They all contain quinolizidine alkaloids – moderately hazardous neurotoxins which can cause vomiting, nausea, dizziness, staggering and coma.

Fir club moss *(Huperzia selago) Cnwp-fwsogl mawr*

This club moss is usually dark green with upright stems and needle-like leaves. Some people say it resembles a tiny conifer. It is very stiff, and sometimes forks near the top. It is occasionally found in grass on dry heathland, but because it is easily dislodged by sheep (and walkers), it has largely retreated to inaccessible areas, and is more common in rocky places such as scree and crags.

Alpine club moss. © Graham Motley

Alpine club moss *(Diphasiastrum alpinium)* ***Cnwp-fwsogl Alpaidd***
This club moss is very rare but can sometimes be found on moors and mountains. It is a dull, greyish-green – a glaucous colour that distinguishes it from all other club mosses – with abundant short branches and leaves that are pressed together.

Stag's horn club moss *(Lycopodium clavatum)* ***Cnwp-fwsogl corn carw***
This club moss prefers sheltered places, such as among the heather on the Blorenge mountain above Abergavenny. The shoots are usually prostrate and branched, with erect, fertile stems which are said to resemble stag's horns (if you have a good imagination!). Unlike the other two species, its leaves end in a short white hair. The spores of this club moss are gathered and sold as lycopodium powder (also called 'vegetable sulphur'), a highly inflammable yellow powder used in fireworks and pharmaceutical processes. Lycopodium spores have the same density as water, and were used to help map the hydrology of the cave systems along the southern edge of the National Park.

Stag's horn club moss. © Julie Bell.

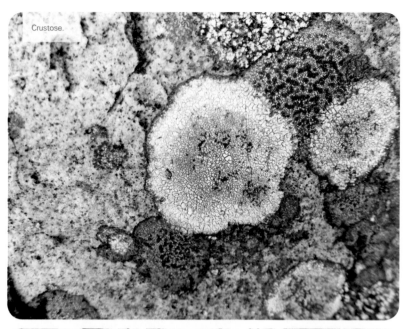

Crustose.

Foliose.

LICHENS / CENNAU

There are tens of thousands of species of lichen, of which almost 2,000 occur in the UK. Although on first glance they appear quite simple, they are actually extremely complex. Far more than just a simple plant, lichens are actually a composite organism: a single entity created by a symbiotic partnership between algae and fungi. The fungi provide shelter for the algae, and in return, the algae provide sustenance for the fungi. Although they are extremely tough and long-lived organisms, found at all heights and all latitudes right across the planet, most require clean air and some are seriously affected by pollution. Given its size, Wales has the highest diversity of lichen species in the world, and they thrive in the clean air of the Brecon Beacons National Park.

Lichens are notoriously difficult to identify, often requiring microscopic investigation and chemical tests, so a detailed examination is way beyond the scope of this book. However, the vast majority of species fall into one of four basic growth types: crustose, foliose, squamulose and fruticose.

Crustose lichen are flat and often resemble splotches of paint. They are usually found on rocks, to which they are tightly attached.

Foliose lichen are plate-like or leafy and are often found on trees. Although they grow flat on their host surface, they are usually not tightly attached.

Squamulose. © Sam Bosanquet.

Fruticose. © Sam Bosanquet.

Squamulose lichens are like an intermediate between crustose and foliose lichens, comprising tight, scale-like clusters of small, overlapping *squamules*. They can be distinguished from foliose lichens by the lack of skin on the underside of the squamules.

Fruticose lichens resemble tiny, multi-branched shrubs and are beloved by model makers who use them for miniature vegetation. Although they may be relatively large, they are often attached to their host surface at a single point.

Just to complicate matters, there are also Placodioid, Leprose and Filamentous lichens, but if you want to find out more about these, you'll have to look in a more specialist book!

Many lichens produce pigments that can be used as dyes, and there is clear evidence that lichens were used to make purple and red dyes as long as two millennia ago. Some lichens produce toxins that kill bacteria, and many are used in traditional medicine where they are given common names like 'lungwort'. Some metabolites produced by lichens have structural and functional similarities to broad-spectrum antibiotics and antiseptics.

Rather than attempt to identify individual species, I have included broad descriptions of some of the more common lichen groups (genera) below.

Caloplaca

There are many species of *Caloplaca*, some with common names like gold lichen, firedot lichen, and jewel lichen. They are sometimes referred to as orange lichens… but they are not always orange, nor are they the only orange lichens! All are crustose, and some have heavily lobed margins with almost parallel furrows. Although they mostly occur in coastal environments, some species can be found on calcareous rocks in upland areas.

Caloplaca.

Cladonia

There are numerous species of *Cladonia* lichen, many of which are difficult to differentiate. Broadly speaking they can be divided into the *cladonia* morpho-type and the *cladina* morpho-type.

The **cladonia** morpho-type (for example pixie cup and devil's matchstick) contains the most species and comprises a group of squamulose lichens with short stalks (or 'podetia'), which vary in size from a few millimetres to a couple of centimetres. Where the podetia end in a cup, they are commonly known as 'pixie cup lichens'. However, the podetia can also taper to a point, often with bright red or orange fruiting bodies (or 'apothecia'), giving rise to common names such as 'Devil's matchstick' and 'British soldier'.

The **cladina** morpho-types (for example reindeer moss) form dense mats of intricate branches, and it is the intricate nature of the branches that is most distinctive, rather than the density. They are sometimes called 'forage lichens', and include a group commonly known as 'reindeer moss'.

Some species of *Cladonia* produce compounds that are used to create antibiotic creams, while others produce metabolites that have been shown to kill leukaemia cells and may therefore have value in the treatment of certain cancers.

Evernia

Evernia (or 'oakmoss') is a bushy lichen, often found on the branches of trees and shrubs. It's very sensitive to ammonia and other nitrogen compounds, therefore is not found in environments that have been enriched by agriculture or polluted by traffic fumes. It has a regular forked appearance, is green on top and white underneath, and becomes very soft when wet. It is widely used in the perfume and cosmetics industries where it is used as a fixative agent to increase shelf-life.

Lepraria

Lepraria is a genus of powdery, pale grey to distinctly blue-grey crustose lichens which form a thin, crust like covering like splodges of dusty paint. They are commonly called dust lichens.

Cladonia – cladonia, e.g. pixie cup / devil's matchstick. © Julie Bell.

Cladonia – cladina, e.g. reindeer moss.

Leprana.

Evernia.

Ochrolechia – cudbear.

Ochrolechia

Also known as cudbear or orchil lichen, *Ochrolechia* is a grey crustose lichen, commonly found covering rocks in upland areas. It is used in the production of cudbear dye, which is used to produce various shades of purple and crimson in woollen and silken fabrics.

Parmelia

Parmelia is a genus of foliose lichens with medium to large leaf-like lobes. These often have a network of white lines or grooves on their surface, with a dark, almost black underside. Sometimes the central area will die away, leaving a ring. Some species of *Parmelia* were once considered to have medicinal properties and were traditionally used in the treatment of epilepsy and plague. Other species have been used to produce a reddish-brown dye for woollen cloth, while *Parmelia perlata* (aka Black Stone Flower) is used as a spice which imparts an unmistakable flavour. *Parmelia* has recently been divided into several different genera, and *Parmelia perlata* is now more correctly known as *Parmotrema perlatum*.

Rhizocarpon

This genus of crustose lichens grows incredibly slowly and survives for thousands of years. It is believed that examples of map lichen *(Rhizocarpus geographicum)* found in the arctic are 8,600 years old, making them by far the oldest living organisms on the planet. Often appearing as a flat patch bordered by black lines, this lichen can sometimes look like a map or a patchwork of fields. Samples of this lichen were once taken into orbit where they were exposed to space conditions for ten days. When they were examined on their return to Earth, they showed minimal damage.

When the patches are circular, this lichen can be used to help determine the age of deposits such as moraines or to determine for how long an outcrop has been exposed, thus revealing evidence of glacial advances. This is done by comparing the size of patches on rocks of a known age (such as on buildings or gravestones, or on quarried faces) with patches of lichen on rocks of an unknown age (such as in moraine deposits or rock outcrops). The process is termed lichenometry.

Although map lichen is one of the better-known species, not all *Rhizocarpon* lichens look like maps. However, most form a bright to greenish-yellow crust that cracks into angular sections separated by flat, black lines.

Usnea

The delicate, bushy, thread-like *Usnea* is common in the ancient woodlands of the National Park, where it hangs from tree branches – hence its common names: old man's beard, beard lichen, and tree-moss. Most species are sensitive to ammonia, nitrogen and sulphur dioxide, so it is generally only found growing in clean air environments. *Usnea* is edible and contains high levels of vitamin C and glucose. It has been used in traditional medicine for at least 1,000 years, particularly in the treatment of uterine disorders and haemorrhage. Usnic acid, which is found in most species, has strong antibiotic and antifungal properties.

The distinctive 'string of sausages' lichen *(Usnea articulata)* has recently colonised the National Park following reductions in sulphur dioxide pollution and has been reported from the ffridd of Mynydd Du in the west to the Sugarloaf and Blorenge in the east.

Parmelia.

Rhizocarpon.

Usnea. © Sam Bosanquet.

Usnea articulata. © Sam Bosanquet.

Blackening wax cap. © Julie Bell.

Bog bell. © Julie Bell.

FUNGI / FFYNGAU

There are about 30,000 different species of fungi in the UK, 10 or 12 of which are really worth eating, and 10 or 12 of which are absolutely poisonous. Despite what many people believe, it is white mushrooms that are responsible for the majority of mushroom poisonings around the world and telling the difference between the edible and the lethally toxic can be extremely difficult. I strongly advise against tasting any fungus unless you have a positive identification from an expert.

Fungi are neither plants nor animals, belonging instead to their own kingdom. Some scientists consider them to be closer to animals than plants, so perhaps they should really be in the next section of the book! Below is a selection of the more common fungi you may see in the uplands or along the upland edge.

Blackening wax cap *(Hygrocybe conica)* *Cap cwyr duol*

Despite their name, these can be red, orange or yellow when young, although they turn jet black with age and then last for a long time, so it is sometimes possible to find all the colours in a single group. Also known as Witch's Hat, many remain conical although some flatten with age. One of the earliest species to appear on sheep-grazed hillsides, they can be seen from late summer into autumn, particularly after rain.

Bog bell *(Galerina paludosa)*

There are many small orange-brown fungi that grow in acid bogs, most of which are indistinguishable to the layman. Bog bell, however, is an exception – it can be identified by its white-edged, ochre-coloured gills, and long stem speckled with white, flaky scales. In addition to sphagnum bogs, it also grows in mossy woodland, and can be found from May to October. Being of the same genus as the deadly 'Death Cap', it is inadvisable to eat it.

Common ink cap *(Coprinopsis atramentaria)* **Cap inc**

The common ink cap is a teetotaller's fungus … it is toxic when consumed with alcohol and can cause severe symptoms even if the alcohol was consumed three days previously! A strong mushroom that can literally lift paving slabs, it is more common to find it in small clusters on the stumps or part-buried logs of deciduous hardwood trees from May to November. This fungus starts egg-shaped then opens to become bell-shaped before deliquescing (liquefying) from the rim upwards. It can be various shades of grey, often shiny and smooth but with small brownish scales near the centre of the 4–7cm diameter cap. The stems are 10–20cm long.

Field mushroom *(Agaricus campestris)* **Madarch y maes**

The most commonly eaten wild mushroom in Britain, field mushrooms sometimes appear in huge quantities in summer and early autumn and can grow to 10cm across. However, they are not quite as straightforward to identify as some people believe. While most are smooth and white, others are rough with dark-brown scales, and although they often occur singly or in small groups, they can also form Fairy Rings. They have a robust flavour which makes them ideal for risottos and omelettes, tasty soups and in meat stews and casseroles.

Common ink cap.

Field mushroom. © Julie Bell

Fly agaric.

Fly agaric *(Amanita muscaria) Amanita'r gwybed*

Arguably the most famous and instantly recognisable fungus, Fly agaric is the classic fairy toadstool. It is notoriously hallucinogenic, but it also contains toxins that cause very unpleasant effects including nausea, sweating and dizziness. It often grows in groups and is particularly common in birch or spruce woodland from August to November. When it first emerges, it is almost entirely covered in white flakes, but as it grows the red skin becomes more prominent, and heavy rain or passing animals can eventually remove all the flakes. When fully open it can grow to 20cm across. The common name refers to its use as an insecticide, in which the fungus is steeped in milk which is then left to attract house flies.

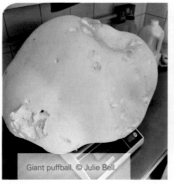

Giant puffball. © Julie Bell.

Golden spindles. © Julie Bell.

Giant puffball *(Calvatia gigantea)* **coden fwg enfawr**

If you come across one of these huge beauties, note the location because they grow year after year and sometimes even form huge fairy rings. They can grow to 80cm diameter and weigh several kilograms. Although they have very little flavour of their own, they are edible if cooked, and are good at soaking up other flavours in soups and stews. Thin strips can be used as a styptic dressing to stem bleeding, and smouldering lumps of puffball have been used by beekeepers to calm the bees and lessen the chances of being stung. They are most commonly found from July to November at the edges of fields and among nettles and vegetation in nutrient-rich waste ground, along woodland edges, and occasionally in woodland clearings.

Golden spindles *(Clavulinopsis fusiformis)*

This common 'fairy club' fungus is quite distinctive, with dense clumps of golden-yellow, unbranched wavy 'spindles' up to 12cm tall. It can be found in acid grassland and woodland clearings from July to November. It is variously described as edible and inedible … so probably best not to eat it!

Honey fungus.

Jelly ear. © Julie Bell.

Honey fungus *(Armillaria mellea)* *Ffwng melog*

This invasive, parasitic fungus does immense damage to a wide range of plant life, particularly trees, and by the time the fruit bodies are visible (usually between July and November) the internal damage is usually fatal. It starts by attacking the living plant, then hangs around to feed on the rotting remains! The cap is brownish-yellow, up to 12cm across, often with tiny light-brown scales, and the gills are slightly bioluminescent, although the light emissions are usually too low to be visible in an outdoor setting, even on a moonless night.

Jelly ear *(Auricularia auricula-judae)* *Ffwng clust*

Mainly seen in winter and spring, this strange fungus grows mainly on dead elder trees, although it can occasionally be found as a weak parasite on the trunks of living elders, and rarely on other broadleaf trees including sycamore, beech and ash. Known also as wood ear and Judas' ear, it is brown with a purple tinge, has a jelly-like texture, and is capable of reconstituting itself when wetted after desiccation. It is edible and is considered a delicacy in China. It can grow to 10cm across.

King Alfred's cakes *(Daldinia concentrica)* ***Peli Duon / Cacenni y Brenin Alfred***

This hard, inedible fungus can be seen throughout the year on ash and beech, and occasionally on other hardwood trees, where it can cause a soft rot. Named after its similarity to burnt cakes, it appears as dark brown to black balls up to 7cm in diameter. It is also known as 'cramp balls' because carrying it was believed to cure cramp, and when dried, it can be used as a fire-lighter – a spark will ignite the flesh which burns slowly and can be used to set flame to dry kindling.

King Alfred's cakes. © Julie Bell.

Magic mushroom. © Graham Motley.

Meadow puffball.

Shaggy parasol – toxic! © Julie Bell.

Parasol.

Magic mushroom *(Psilocybe semilanceata)* **Madarch hud**

Known as 'liberty cap' in the USA, the magic mushroom is legally a Class A drug. It appears in upland grassland in late summer and autumn and is rarely more than 8cm high, with a conical cap up to 1.5cm across, and a sharp central pip. It contains the toxin, psilocybin, which in addition to its hallucinogenic properties, also causes vomiting and anxiety attacks. It is not as easy to identify as some people think ... a fact that results in several cases of mushroom poisoning each year!

Meadow puffball *(Lycoperdon pratense)*

This is one of the more common puffball fungi found in grassland along the upland edge from June to October, and although it can be mistaken for a baby giant puffball, it can be distinguished because it has a stump-like stem whereas the giant puffball has none. Although it is edible when young, it can bear a striking resemblance to earth balls, which are inedible and can cause serious poisoning. If it is dark brown or black inside, it's not a puffball! It grows to 8cm wide and 4cm tall.

Parasol *(Macrolepiota procera)* **Ambarelo'r bwgan**

This beautiful fungus is found from July to November in neglected pasture-land, in grassy areas along the wooded upland edge and in woodland clearings, either alone or in small groups. The scaly white or buff cap can grow to 25cm across, with a smooth brownish-red central 'umbo'. The stems are up to 30cm long with a snakeskin pattern and a collar that can sometimes become detached and slide down. Although edible, care is needed as it can be confused with the shaggy parasol, which is toxic and can cause severe allergic reaction. The shaggy parasol can be distinguished as its flesh turns red when cut, and its stem lacks the snakeskin-like patterning.

Pleated ink cap *(Parasola plicatilis)*

This graceful little ink cap is sometimes called the 'little Japanese umbrella' for reasons that are obvious when you see it! The pale grey cap is 1–2cm wide, heavily ribbed with a distinctive yellowish-brown centre, and the stem can be up to 6cm long. Initially egg-shaped, it slowly flattens with age but is very short-lived, appearing at dawn after a wet night, opening fully by lunchtime, and then shrivelling to nothing by evening. It is seen from May to November, most often in small groups in short grass along the upland edge, but sometimes in woodland glades.

Scarlet elf cup *(Sarcoscypha austriaca)*

This distinctive fungus appears in winter, particularly in woodland where there is plenty of moss and fallen branches, although it can also occasionally be found along the banks of streams or ditches. The circular or oval cups are bright red, up to 5cm across and 2cm tall. Some books say it is edible while others say it is not, but it is certainly eaten by rodents and slugs!

Shaggy ink cap *(Coprinus comatus)* Cap inc carpiog

Also known as lawyer's wig, this distinctive ink cap can grow to 6cm in diameter and 15cm tall. It is most commonly found in summer and autumn, in open woodland and along the wooded upland edge, usually in small groups but occasionally in lines or fairy rings. Like many fungi, it is most abundant soon after rain. These ink caps are edible when young, but the gills turn black as they age, eventually deliquescing (liquefying) from the rim upwards to leave a tiny black disc perched on top of a dying stem.

Snowy wax cap *(Cuphophyllus virgineus)* Cap cwyr

Fairly common in sheep-cropped upland acid grassland from August to November, this small ivory-coloured wax cap can also sometimes be found in woodland clearings. It is usually found in small groups or 'tufts' and can be distinguished from other pale wax caps by its very widely spaced gills. It can grow to 4cm across and 5cm high, flattening or even becoming funnel-shaped with age.

Pleated ink cap.

Scarlet elf cup. © Julie Bell.

Shaggy ink cap. © Julie Bell.

Snowy wax cap.

Stinkhorn *(Phallus impudicus)* *Pidyn Drewllyd*

You will probably smell this fungus before you see it – and once smelt, you will never forget it! During the summer months, the 'horn' grows from an egg-shaped fungus that hides beneath leaf-litter in woodlands, especially coniferous woodlands where there are rotting stumps or dead wood. The horn is covered with a very smelly olive-green ooze that is soon eaten by insects to reveal a white honeycombed core. It can grow to 25cm tall.

Stinkhorn. © Julie Bell.

Sulphur tuft.

Velvet shank. © Julie Bell.

Wax caps.

Sulphur tuft *(Hypholoma fasciculare)* **Torthau'r tylwyth teg**

These bright yellow, wood-rotting fungi are particularly spectacular, growing in dense clumps on fallen or hollow trees and decaying stumps from May to November. These 'tufts' can recur on the same site for several years until the wood is well rotted. If you see them on grass, you will probably find some wood buried just below the surface. Up to 10cm tall, the caps can grow to 8cm across and often darken towards the centre. They are poisonous, and eating them can result in severe stomach pains, temporary paralysis and distorted vision.

Velvet shank *(Flammulina velutipes)* **Coesyn melfed**

One of the few fungi that can be seen in the depths of winter, this has clusters of golden-brown caps that darken towards the centre. Slimy in wet weather, the caps dry to a smooth sheen and can survive sub-zero temperatures. A stump-rotting variety, it is particularly common on beech, although it can also be found on other dead or diseased hardwood trees. It is edible and is grown commercially in Japan where it is known as Enoki. Like many fungi, the initially bell-shaped cap flattens with age. It can grow to 8cm wide and 10cm high, although the caps are often distorted because of the density of the cluster.

Wax caps *(Hygrocybe)* **Capia cwyr**

Wax caps come in a vast range of different sizes and colours, from red and orange to purple and black. I have described two species – blackening wax cap and snowy wax cap – in slightly more detail above, but the range here is enormous. In fact, the Brecon Beacons National Park is internationally important for wax cap fungi as 60% of the UK wax caps are found here. Wax caps are killed by phosphate fertilisers and other chemical enrichment, so their presence here is an indicator of environmental quality. The more wax caps there are, the higher the environmental standing. Although many of the larger wax caps are relatively easy to identify, several of the smaller species are extremely difficult to distinguish, and some have wide variation in colour and size. Whatever their scientific name, it is still easy to appreciate their bizarre beauty.

Bracken.

Bracken.

FERNS / RHEDYN

One of the simplest and most ancient groups of plants on earth, ferns have been around for at least 360 million years and can be found in different habitats all over the world. At one time they were the dominant vegetation, and today there are about 12,000 species globally. Some of these have existed unchanged for at least 180 million years, but many are more recent, appearing after the emergence of flowering plants roughly 145 million years ago. Although not of major economic importance, ferns have been used as a source of fibres, dyes and drugs, as biofuels, biofertilisers and ornamental plants, and they have also been the subject of research into their ability to remove chemical pollutants from the atmosphere and con-taminated soil. Some species have been used as food, but identification is important as others (such as bracken) have been found to be mutagenic and carcinogenic, and many contain insecticides.

Bracken *(Pteridium aquilinum) Rhedynen ungoes*

A fern that most walkers will immediately recognise, bracken often dominates the lower flanks of hills and neglected fields at the upland edge. It is unusual to find it on the highest ground because it's frost sensitive. Unlike many ferns, it dies back in winter leaving brown withered fronds, reappearing in spring when the tightly curled new fronds push through the ground and unfurl. Originally a lowland and woodland plant, it is a very successful coloniser that became invasive following tree clearance and increased sheep grazing. The dense foliage shades out other vegetation, and the deep litter layer also prevents other species from becoming established. It is becoming a major problem plant on many hillsides, particularly in the Black Mountains.

Bracken was once harvested for animal bedding, as a mulch for potatoes, as a soil improver, and as a source of potash for glassmaking. In the 17th century it was highly sought after during times of drought as it was believed that burning it would cause rain. However, all parts of the plant are poisonous, and the fronds are most toxic when young. It is therefore important that bracken cut for animal bedding has died back entirely. The plant is also considered a hazard to human health due not only to its carcinogenic spores, but also because it provides a good habitat for sheep ticks that transmit Lyme's disease.

Brittle bladder-fern *(Cystopteris fragilis) Ffiolredynen frau*

This delicate little deciduous fern has fronds up to 30cm long and is mostly found in rock crevices on upland limestone and in cracks in stone walls. It gets its name from the inflated bladder-like bag that covers its rounded spores. A decoction of the roots has been used as an enema to get rid of parasitic worms.

Green spleenwort *(Asplenium viride) Glas-wallt y forwyn*

This small evergreen fern is found mainly in crevices on limestone pavements and upland limestone outcrops, especially in the central and western parts of the Park. It is commonly mis-identified as maidenhair spleenwort, although it can be easily distinguished by the fact that the mid-rib supporting its leaflets is a uniform green colour whereas the mid-rib in maidenhair fern is brown or black.

Green spleenwort.

Brittle bladder-fern.

Hard fern.

Hart's tongue fern.

Hard fern *(Blechnum spicant)* *Rhedyn bras*

Also known as deer fern, this medium-sized fern is common in acidic oak woods and other acidic habitats, where it prefers deep shade rather than full sunshine. Its fronds grow to about 40cm long, and it remains green for most of the year. In herbal medicine, the leaflets have been chewed in the treatment of stomach problems, and the fronds are used externally as a medicine for skin sores. A decoction of the root has been used in the treatment of diarrhoea.

Hart's tongue fern *(Asplenium scolopendrium)* *Tafod yr hydd*

This widespread evergreen fern is very simple, the frond being just a single shiny, green tongue-shaped leaf up to 50cm long. It is most abundant in ash woodland, particularly on limestone, and in hedges. The underside of the leaf has little marks that look a bit like centipedes' legs, hence the species name *scolopendrium* – the Latin for centipede! The fronds have many medicinal uses. They can be used in ointments for the treatment of piles, burns and scalds, and an infusion can be taken for the treatment of diarrhoea.

Lemon-scented fern *(Oreopteris limbosperma)* **Marchredyn y Mynydd**

A common fern of the uplands, especially on rocky slopes below crags in acidic habitats, this tufted fern is yellowish-green with fronds up to 100cm long, widest at their centre, and very narrow at their base. Many ferns look similar, and this is no exception ... but crush the leaf and there is a mild though distinct smell of lemon.

Limestone fern *(Gymnocarpium robertianum)* **Llawredynen y Calchfaen**

Although usually a scarce plant, this deciduous fern is abundant at a few sites in the central and eastern areas of the Park. It grows in warm, sunny spots on limestone scree and in cracks and fissures in limestone rock. It first appears with its fronds curled into a tiny ball, then it slowly unfurls into separate small fists, and then into solitary, erect, triangular leaves. It is never tufted or arranged in a crown.

Maidenhair spleenwort *(Asplenium trichomanes)* **Duegredynen gwallt y forwyn**

Easily recognisable, maidenhair spleenwort has fronds made up of short, round leaflets paired from a central brown or black stem up to 20cm long. It is evergreen and grows in tufts on limestone rocks, old mortared walls and mossy branches. A sweet tea can be made from the fronds ... but be careful as it can have laxative properties. It has also been used in the treatment of chest complaints and to promote menstruation.

Male fern *(Dryopteris)* **Marchredyn**

Male ferns are one of a number of similar species (including Buckler ferns and Lady fern) which are difficult to tell apart. Common in deciduous woodland, hedges and cliffs, it forms large shuttlecock-shaped clumps up to 80cm high. The bright green fronds unfurl from scaly brown underground rhizomes in mid spring. Each frond is separated into deeply divided, tapering leaflets which grow from the main stem in opposite pairs. These form impressive stands in the summer but die back later in the year. In herbal medicine, it provides one of the most popular and effective treatments for tape worms.

Lemon-scented fern.

Limestone fern.

Maidenhair spleenwort.

Male fern.

Polypodies *(Polypodium)* **Marchredyn y dŵr**

Polypodies are medium-sized ferns, often found on old walls and crags, and common on mossy trees. They particularly like humid oak woods such as those in the west of the Park and the Waterfall Country. There are three similar-looking species, all with ladder-like fronds up to 50cm in length, with finger-like leaflets coming out of the main stem. The root is very sweet and is used as a liquorice adulterant. It is traditionally used as a laxative, as a treatment for hepatitis and jaundice, and as a remedy for indigestion and loss of appetite.

Rustyback *(Ceterach officinarum)* **Duegredynen gefngoch**

These beautiful, small evergreen ferns are most often seen on old walls but can also be found on limestone crags. On first glance they can be mistaken for spleenwort, but the fronds, which can grow to 12cm, are green on top and rust red underneath. Unlike most other ferns, they like plenty of sun, and if they dry out during a dry spell, they soon rehydrate after wetting.

Shield ferns *(Polystichum)* **Gwrychredyn**

There are many species of shield fern and lots of hybrids! Most are evergreen or semi-evergreen, with short stout rhizomes and have pinnately divided fronds in neat shuttlecock-like rosettes that can grow to a metre in height. They are mainly found in limestone woodlands but can also be found on rocky slopes below ORS cliffs where there is some calcareous influence. An infusion of the fronds can be used as a hair rinse and to treat dandruff.

Polypodies.

Rustyback.

Shield ferns.

Mat grass (and inset).

Purple moor grass (and inset).

GRASSES, RUSHES AND SEDGES

There are 54 genera and 160 species of grass in Britain, 109 genera and 5,500 species of sedge, and just 2 genera of rush. I am not going to attempt to describe them in detail as many of them look remarkably similar! They are all wind pollinated, which means the plant has no need of showy petals with which to attract insects, so the flowers are often reduced or absent.

The three types can be distinguished as follows:

Stems

Although there are one or two exceptions, grasses have hollow stems, rushes have solid, round stems, and sedges have solid, angular stems. Grass stems usually have nodes or joints whereas sedges and rushes do not. Grasses often produce both vegetative and floral stems whereas sedges and rushes develop only floral stems.

Leaves

Grasses usually have leaves arranged in two rows on either side of the stems, and the leaf sheath (the part of the leaf that enfolds the stem) is typically open. Sedge leaves are usually found along the stem in three vertical planes, whereas rush leaves are usually found at the base of the stem and arranged in a spiral. However this varies among different species. The leaf sheath of rushes and sedges is typically closed.

Flowers and fruit

Grasses produce relatively showy flowers whereas sedges and rushes usually have inconspicuous flowers. The fruits are usually easier to distinguish than the flowers. The fruits of grasses vary greatly and include large 'kernels' and tiny oval seeds. Sedges produce 2.5cm-long prickly, beak-shaped fruit clusters. Rushes produce tiny round fruits, less than 3mm in diameter.

Grasses and rushes can either be annuals or perennials, whereas all sedges are perennial.

The wide expanses of uniform hillside that typify the uplands of the Brecon Beacons are commonly called 'white moors' and are characterised by **mat grass** *(Nardus stricta) Cawnen ddu* and **purple moor-grass** *(Molinia caerulea) Glaswellt y gweunydd*, two species which dominate to such an extent that they have a detrimental effect on biodiversity. Dry-looking mat grass is coarse and tufted and tends to dominate in drier ground. Its dominance indicates that sheep grazing levels have been high in the past. Purple-moor grass prefers the damp and can dominate in extensive areas of wet ground where it often forms large tussocks (which can make walking difficult).

The ffridd more commonly has **common bent** *(Agrostis capillaris) maeswellt cyffredin* and **sheep's fescue** *(Festuca ovina) peiswellt y defaid.*

Common bent (and below).

Sheep's fescue.

Red fescue.

Where the soil is alkaline, such as along the limestone outcrops, these species are joined by **red fescue** *(Festuca rubra) peiswellt coch* and **quaking grass** *(Briza media) crydwellt.*

On boggy, less well drained areas such as can be found in Rhôs pasture, the vegetation is often dominated by rushes – particularly **jointed rush** *(Juncus articulatus) brwynen gymalog,* **sharp-flowered rush** (Juncus acutiflorus) brwynen flodfain, and **soft rush** *(Juncus effuses) brwynen babwyr.* Where the very coarse **heath rush** *(Juncus squarrosus) brwynen droellgorun* occurs, this probably indicates areas that were once wet heathland.

Quaking grass.

Jointed rush.

Sharp-flowered rush.

Soft rush (and right).

Heath rush (and right).

Winter wimberry.
Inset: wimberry without leaves.

Foxglove leaves.

FLOWERS / BLODAU

There are about 850 species of flowering plants native to the Brecon Beacons National Park. I've only included a few of them here, but I have tried to list the more common. In an attempt to help you identify those that you see, I've divided this section into three broad habitats – uplands, wet and boggy areas, and woodlands and hedgerows. These divisions are fairly arbitrary as many plants occur across the range or spread into neighbouring habitats.

These plants are here for everyone to enjoy, so please do not pick any. It is actually illegal to uproot any wild plant without the landowner's consent, and it is also a criminal offence to collect seeds or flowers from protected species. Where I have mentioned medicinal or culinary uses, these are given purely for interest and not as suggestions or recommendations! It is not a good idea to eat or even taste any plant without a positive identification, as some are extremely poisonous.

Upland habitats

Upland is defined as land above the level of agricultural enclosure. The uplands of the Brecon Beacons National Park comprise not just one habitat but several, including open and rocky mountainside, rough acid grassland, and moorland and heath. There are also some important limestone pavements, plus an important but vague zone sandwiched between the uplands and the lowlands, known in Wales as ffridd.

Open and rocky hillside.

Rough acid grassland.

Heather moor.

Cottongrass moor.

Wimberry moor.

Purple moor grass and rush pasture.

Large areas of the upland are wet and boggy, as described in the next section.

Open and rocky mountainside

The gentle, open mountainsides of the Brecon Beacons make them a magnet for walkers, but there is far more here than just heather, grass and wimberry. The stunning north-facing ORS escarpment that snakes across the northern part of the Park supports a number of rare arctic-alpine plants, and the upland limestone cliffs support a characteristic flora, which is unusual in Wales.

Rough acid grassland

Upland acid grassland is dominated by grasses and herbs and is found on lime-deficient soils formed from acid rocks, such as sandstones, or from superficial deposits such as glacial till. The large expanses of uniform hillside (commonly called 'white moors') are dominated by mat-grass, which is so unpalatable that sheep leave it alone, instead grazing everything else in the area. This results in a habitat that is typically species-poor. On wetter ground, rushes predominate.

Moorland and heath

Heather or ling dominated moorland is not as common as many people think, although there are sizable areas on the Carmarthen Fans and Fforest Fawr, and on some of the eastern hills such as the Black Mountains and the Blorenge. Dry heath typically has ling and bilberry, while wetter heath has cross-leaved heath and purple moor-grass. Although most commonly associated with heather, there are actually several different types of moorland:
fescue and mat grass moor (the 'rough acid grassland' described previously); cottongrass moor;
heather moor and upland heath;
bilberry (or wimberry) moor and upland heath;
purple moor grass and rush pasture.
All can be found within the National Park, and although it can be argued that the latter type is predominantly a lowland habitat, it does occur in places on the upland fringe (see also *ffridd* overleaf and *rhôs pasture* on page 131).

Limestone pavement

Limestone pavements (see also page 42) are special places with a diverse plant life. They provide a unique habitat which has developed slowly over millions of years, yet the vast majority have been irretrievably damaged by the removal of stone. There are about 20 hectares of limestone pavement in the National Park, and although on first sight they may appear barren, the fissures, or 'grikes', provide shelter for plants more typical of the lowlands. Where pavements have been left ungrazed, woodland has developed over them, providing yet another habitat.

Ffridd

The ffridd zone is a vague region containing various habitats that occur at the interface of upland and lowland. It is found almost exclusively on slopes, particularly in those areas where it is difficult to farm due to steepness, rock outcrops or boulders. Its boundaries are difficult to define as it often merges into more clearly-defined upland habitats above and lowland pastures below. It is thus a dynamic edge zone, sometimes displaying successive stages in the development of woodland from grassland or heathland, but more often (in this area at least) providing species with the opportunity to make vertical movements as they compensate for climate change. There are often extensive areas of bracken with pockets of dry heath and acid grassland, a few flushes (see page 131), and a scattering of scrub such as hawthorn, gorse, blackthorn and holly. Where larger trees occur, they are usually birch and mountain ash, with maybe the occasional ash or oak.

Limestone pavement.

Ffridd.

Autumn gentian. © Graham Motley.

Barren strawberry (and inset). © Julie Bell.

Autumn gentian *(Gentianella amarella)* **Crwynllys yr hydref**

Although quite a rare plant, this can often be found on limestone pavements and upland limestone grasslands in August. A late-flowering biennial, it has spikes of four- or five-petalled purple blooms and narrow, red-tinged pointed leaves in opposite pairs on the stem. It sometimes grows in large groups. Gentians contain compounds which are nowadays best known as ingredients of bitter alcoholic drinks. It has long been used as a herbal bitter in the treatment of digestive disorders, and has been used in the past to treat malaria

Barren strawberry *(Potentilla sterilis)* **Llwyn coeg-fefus**

Despite what the name may suggest, the barren strawberry is not a strawberry at all, but a member of a completely different genus! Although easily mistaken for a wild strawberry, it can be distinguished by its flower. Wild strawberry has a yellow dome in the middle of the flower, whereas barren strawberry does not. The flowers are also slightly different, with the petals of barren strawberry being wider apart. It is one of the earliest plants to flower and is common on dry grassy banks, in rocky crevices and in woods. It does not produce delicious fruit like wild strawberry.

Heath bedstraw (and inset). © Julie Bell.

Bell heather.

Bedstraws *(Galium)*

Bedstraws are in a plant genus containing about 400 species. They are characterised by finely toothed, needle-shaped whorls of leaves, and clusters of small white, yellow or green flowers on square stems. The fruit is often covered in hooked bristles. Many have a spreading or sprawling habit, and several can scramble. Historically, many species were used to stuff mattresses, hence their common name. They were also strewn on stone floors to sweeten the air, used to make a red dye, and they are valued by herbalists.

Heath bedstraw *(Galium saxatile) Briwydden wen* is common in acid grassland. A mat-forming leafy perennial, it grows best on dry, grassy, acid soils where it produces masses of tiny white four-petalled flowers in loose branching clusters from June to August. It has a sweet but sometimes sickly smell.

Limestone bedstraw *(Galium sterneri) Briwydden y garreg galch* is usually quite scarce but is locally frequent on limestone grassland and pavements in the Park. Unless you are an expert, it looks almost identical to heath bedstraw!

See also common marsh bedstraw and fen bedstraw on page 132, and common cleavers on page 146.

Bird's-foot trefoil (and inset).

Common mouse ear. © Julie Bell.

Bell heather *(Erica cinerea)* *Grug y mêl*

You will only find this heather in areas where there are few sheep because the animals seem to love eating it. A distinctive plant, it has clusters of dark purple-pink, bell-shaped flowers and short, dark green needle-like leaves in whorls of three. It is evergreen, but really comes to life between July and September when the flowers appear, attracting lots of bees. It particularly likes dry, well-drained areas.

Bird's-foot trefoil *(Lotus corniculatus)* *Pysen-y-ceirw*

Found on grassland and limestone pavements, bird's-foot trefoil is a member of the pea family. It has bunches of 2–5 bright yellow flowers (sometimes tinged with red) on a wiry stalk. Although it looks as if there are only two petals, there are in fact five. Its seed pods resemble a bird's claw – hence its common name. It is also known as 'granny's toenails', 'eggs and bacon', 'butter and eggs', and 'hen and chickens'. It is an important source of nectar for pollinating insects, and although it is poisonous to humans, it is used as a forage plant for livestock. An orange-yellow dye is obtained from the flowers.

Common mouse ear *(Cerastium fontanum)* *Clust-y-llygoden gulddail*

A low-growing, spreading plant, common mouse-ear is a type of chickweed with tiny, white, five-petalled flowers and dark green leaves covered with white hairs. It flowers from April to September and is found in a range of upland habitats. Its seeds can survive in the soil for up to 40 years, and it has been found in prehistoric deposits.

Crowberry *(Empetrum nigrum)* *Creiglys*

The evergreen crowberry is often mistaken for heather, to which it is related. A common sight on moors and damp hillsides, it has very small, needle-like leaves with a white stripe on the reverse, and produces tiny purple star-shaped flowers in April or May, followed by small berries which turn from green through pink and purple to shiny black as the year progresses. Although they are an important food source for birds (particularly grouse), the berries can remain into the winter. They can also be eaten by humans, although it has to be said that they don't taste very nice! Crowberry is known by several other names including crow ling, lingberry, mossberry, berry-gorse, crawcrooks, and she-heather. The leaves and reddish-brown stems are used in traditional Inuit medicine, and the berries have been used to treat scurvy and epilepsy, and to produce a purple dye.

Dog violet *(Viola riviniana)* *Fioled gyffredin*

This is the most common violet you are likely to see, although there are other, similar species. Each stem has a single, unscented flower with five petals, and the leaves are heart-shaped, on long, slender stalks. A rich source of vitamins A and C, violets have an important place in herbal medicine and are considered excellent in the treatment of coughs and colds. The flowers were once made into a conserve called 'violet sugar', which was considered unrivalled in the treatment of consumption (tuberculosis). In folklore, the violet is a symbol of modesty and faithfulness, and is listed as one of the most powerful forces against evil. However, it is considered unlucky to bring a single flower into a house.

Crowberry (and right).

Dog violet.

Goldenrod.

Goldenrod *(Solidago virgaurea) Eurwialen*

Most often seen on ledges on sandstone and gritstone cliffs, this untidy plant has yellow compound flowers, oval leaves and downy stems and can grow up to 50cm high. Herbalists use it as an astringent for treating wounds and bleeding, and a homeopathic remedy made from the plant is used in the treatment of kidney and bladder disorders, rheumatism and arthritis. When made into a tea, it can be used as a mouth rinse for inflammation of the mouth and throat.

Common gorse (and right).

Western gorse (and right).

Common gorse *(Ulex europaeus)* *Eithinen Ffrengig* **and**
western gorse *(Ulex gallii)* *Eithinen mân*

There are three species of gorse in Britain, two of which grow in the Park. **Common gorse** is the more common and usually flowers from January to June, while **western gorse** usually flowers from July to November. Both have vicious spikey leaves and bright yellow flowers with a distinctive co-conut fragrance, and if they flowered at the same time, we'd have difficulty in telling them apart. However, one slight difference is that common gorse tends to be tall and straggly, whereas western gorse tends to be lower growing and more compact. Regarded as a sacred tree by the Celts, a branch of gorse hung over a doorway will protect the house from witches, and you should only kiss your lover when gorse is in flower … which it is pretty much all the time! Before the Industrial Revolution gorse was valued as a fuel for fires and kilns. The bark and flowers produce a fine yellow dye, and the flowers can be used to flavour whiskey and to make beer, wine and tea. In homeopathy gorse is used to fight depression.

Harebell.

Hawkbit.

Hawkweed.

Harebell *(Campanula rotundifolia)* *Clych yr eos*

Common in dry acid grassland, this fragile-looking flower is actually really tough, although it doesn't like being damp. Its delicate blue bell-shaped flowers appear on slender 15–40cm tall stalks in the latter part of summer and are regularly visited by bumblebees and other insects looking for a late source of nectar. Also known as cuckoo's shoe, witch bells and old man's bell, it is used in traditional medicine to treat soreness, particularly of the ears and eyes. Dreaming about harebells signifies true love, and in Celtic mythology it is seen as a fairy plant that is perilous to pick.

Hawkbit *(Leontodon)* *Peradyl* **and hawkweed** *(Hieracium)* *Heboglys*

There are literally hundreds of different hawkbits and hawkweeds in the Park, and even experienced botanists can have difficulty distinguishing them. In addition to some widespread, common ones, there are many rare species here, and some have their entire world population confined to a single rock outcrop. Their bright yellow flowers make them easy to spot, but they are commonly mistaken for dandelions. The easiest way to tell the difference is that dandelions have hollow, leafless, unbranched stems and milky sap, no hairs on the leaves or stems, and only one flower per stem. A member of the daisy family, they have been used by herbalists as a remedy for jaundice and dropsy, and as a diuretic.

Ling / heather *(Calluna vulgaris)* **Grug**

Commonly known as heather, this is one of the last wild plants to flower in summer. It has tiny purple or white flowers from July to October, carried on tough, wiry sprawling stems. Where it is not over-grazed by sheep, it can grow to well over 50cm, which makes walking difficult. In days gone by, heather was often used to make brooms (besoms) for sweeping floors – or for flying by witches! It was also used to stuff bedding, to dye wood and tan leather. In some areas, hives are transported to heather moorland in late summer so that the bees can gather nectar from the flowers and produce delicious heather honey.

Mossy saxifrage *(Saxifraga hypnoides)* **Tormaen mwsoglaidd**

Although usually scarce, saxifrage is fairly common in limestone areas where it grows on rocks, ledges and beside mountain streams and is distinguishable from other similar saxifrages by a spread of twisted narrow, three-forked leaves at ground level which resemble moss. On limestone pavements these leaves can sometimes be reddish in colour. It flowers from May to July, with five white petals on top of a thin stem, and pink-tipped buds branching out on short stalks slightly lower down.

Purple saxifrage *(Saxifraga oppositifolia)* **Tormaen porffor**

If you are lucky you might catch a glimpse of this beautiful plant in early spring. The only saxifrage with purple flowers, it's a low-growing, mat-forming plant with tiny leaves and penny-sized flowers with five slightly sticky, rounded petals. It is rare in the UK, but very common all over the Arctic, and is one of the most northerly growing plants in the world. It has also been found at a height of over 4500m in the Swiss Alps, making it the highest elevation plant of its type in Europe. It likes the cold, so the Brecon Beacons are ideal, and the north-facing escarpment of the Craig Cerrig-gleisiad National Nature Reserve (NNR) is its most southerly recorded British location.

Rue-leaved saxifrage *(Saxifraga tridactylites)* **Tormaen tribys**

Similar to other saxifrages, this particular species can be recognised by its reddish zigzag stems and leaves, both of which are sticky and hairy. The flowers are white, 4–6mm wide, in leafy clusters on stalks up to 15cm long. The leaves are fleshy and have a distinctive three-toed appearance. Although it's usually regarded as a lowland saxifrage, it sometimes grows in bare, dry upland locations such as limestone pavements, and can be found in the Craig y Cilau NNR above Crickhowell.

Ling (and right and below).

Mossy saxifrage.

Purple saxifrage. © Anne Griffiths.

Rue-leaved saxifrage. © Anne Griffiths.

Self-heal *(Prunella vulgaris)* **Y feddyges las**

A common sight in upland grassland, self-heal is a low, creeping plant with dense clusters of bluish or violet flowers from June to October. It often forms a mat, and its purple-tinged seed heads remain well into autumn. Traditionally used in herbal remedies, particularly for sore throats, and still used extensively in Chinese herbal medicine, self-heal has a variety of pharmacological effects and is currently being investigated for use in the treatment of certain cancers.

Snake's-head fritillary *(Fritillaria meleagris)* **Britheg**

Although very rare, Snake's-head fritillaries are unmistakeable, and sightings have been reported around Talgarth, and from the Craig y Cilau NNR near Crickhowell. They have single purple, pink or even white bell-like flowers with a distinctive chequer-board pattern, which dangle downwards from single stalks up to 30cm tall. The narrow, grey-green leaves appear at the base of the plant and occasionally higher up the stem. They have been described as "one of the most exquisite jewels in the treasure house of British wild flowers".

Speedwells *(Veronica)* **Rhwyddlwyn**

This family of wild flowers grows in a wide variety of different habitats. Species typically have tiny blue or lilac flowers and big green leaves, and they mostly flower from May to August. **Heath speedwell** *(Veronica officinalis) rhwyddlwyn meddygol* grows in open woods, grassland and heathland and has small, pale-blue flowers in a tapering, vertical spike, about 10cm high. It was once used as a cure for gout and for making tea. See also brooklime (page 133).

Self-heal (and right).

Snake's-head fritillary (and right). © Julie Bell.

Germander speedwell.

Heath speedwell.

Thistles / *Ysgallen*

The term 'thistle' is often used to describe any plant which has sharp prickles on its leaves, yet there are a vast number of different thistles. They are mostly seen as weeds, and some species contain chemicals that can affect the health of animals that eat more than small amounts of them. However, other species are grown as sources of oil, pharmaceutical compounds and vegetable rennet used in cheese making. **Marsh thistle** *(Cirsium palustre) ysgall y gors* is very common, particularly in the damper areas as its name suggests, where it can grow to well over a metre in height. **Spear thistle** *(Cirsium vulgare) marchysgallen* is the classic thistle – a purple, fluffy-looking flower sitting above a spiny ball – and may well have given rise to the Scottish national emblem. Along with **creeping thistle** *(Circium arvense) ysgallen y maes*, this is most frequent in fields along the upland edge. **Carline thistle** *(Carlina vulgaris) ysgallen siarl* has distinctive golden-brown flower heads and looks a bit like a dying daisy or a thistle that's gone to seed. It is locally frequent in limestone areas, particularly on old lime spoil. In Celtic folklore thistles represent bravery, determination and endurance, and some species are valued in traditional medicine.

Tormentil *(Potentilla erecta) Tresgl y moch*

You will see the bright yellow flowers of tormentil all over the uplands from May onwards – so much so that it is known locally as 'constant companion'. Although it resembles a small buttercup, it can be immediately distinguished as it has only four petals. The plant contains more tannin than oak bark, is strongly astringent and has antibiotic properties. It can be used as a styptic to staunch the bleeding of minor cuts, and it is used widely in herbal medicine as a treatment for diarrhoea, dysentery, irritable bowel syndrome, colitis, toothache, mouth ulcers and infected gums ... to name but a few! The roots are used to produce 'Tormentil Red': a dye for reddening leather, and an ingredient in red ink and artists' colours.

Marsh thistle (and right).

Spear thistle (and right).

Creeping thistle.

Carline thistle.

Tormentil (and right).

Wall pennywort leaves.

Wall pennywort flower spike.

Wall pennywort / navelwort *(Umbilicus rupestris)* ***Deilen gron***

Wall pennywort or navelwort is a very shallow-rooted plant that likes to nestle in damp crevices in shady rocky areas or stone walls and is easily recognised. Its fleshy, succulent green leaves have an obvious depression (or 'navel') in the middle, and the greenish white bell-shaped flowers grow in narrow spikes up to 25cm long. The leaves are edible – best gathered after rain when they are juicy – and they can also be used to ease minor burns and cuts by removing the lower surface and applying the leaf directly to the skin.

Wild strawberry *(Fragaria vesca)* ***Mefus gwyllt***

Common in limestone areas, this plant spreads via long runners, and has glossy, toothed-edged leaves. The white flowers have five petals with a golden centre and appear from April into summer. The unmistakeable red berries follow in July and August, providing a tasty treat if eaten straight from the plant on a sunny day. The leaves and roots can be used to treat inflammation of the bowel and to improve bile and liver function, and the berries are used in traditional medicine as a diuretic and to treat gout. Wild strawberry infusions have been used to treat sore throats.

Wild strawberry.

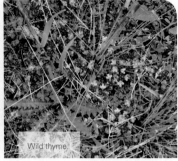
Wild thyme.

Wild thyme *(Thymus polytrichus) Teim gwyllt*

Wild thyme is common in the limestone areas of the Park, sometimes forming low mats which fill the air with fragrance as you walk across them. An aromatic, creeping plant with an unmistakeable scent, it has pairs of tiny oval leaves along its stems, and tightly bunched heads of light-purple flowers. It is the main food of the larva of the large blue butterfly, and sometimes plays host to the tiny thyme gall-mite *(Aceria thomasi) coden teim-gwiddonyn*, which makes its home in a ball of tightly clustered whitish hairs (about 1cm in diameter) surrounding the top leaves. According to folklore, fairies live in patches of thyme and will bless any place where it grows; a pillow stuffed with thyme prevents nightmares and encourages positive dreams; and wearing a sprig of thyme in your hair attracts the opposite sex and makes you irresistible! Herbalists consider it an excellent treatment for coughs and colds, and thyme tea settles the stomach, soothes sore throats, relieves aches and pains, and helps you sleep.

Wimberry with berries.

Wimberry

Purple bird droppings!

Wimberry *(Vaccinium myrtillus)* ***Llus neu lusi duon bach***

Commonly known as bilberry (also whin, winberry, blaeberry and wortle-berry), this small deciduous shrub grows widely on the uplands as well as in some woodlands, and it is often dominant on steeper slopes just above the bracken zone. It has stiff, 15–60cm high stems, and produces lantern-shaped green-pink flowers in spring and deliciously edible blue-black berries in summer. The berries are gobbled up by all sorts of birds, the evidence of which is often seen in the form of purple bird-droppings! They are also very popular with humans, and it is traditional to start collecting wimberries on the last Sunday in July. Wimberry has been used in traditional medicine since the middle ages: the leaf is used to treat diabetes, and the berries for osteoarthritis, chronic fatigue, gout, haemorrhoids, eye ailments and urinary tract infections.

Wet and boggy areas

Wales is renowned for being wet! Although this is arguably a dubious reputation, there are many examples of wetland and boggy terrain across the National Park, including bogs and fens, peat bog and marsh, blanket bog, raised bog, flushes, and rhôs pasture. There are also narrow wetland habitats alongside upland streams and around upland pools and lakes.

Bog or fen?

Bogs are areas of acidic wet ground dominated by the growth of bog mosses such as sphagnum, whereas fens are areas of alkaline wet ground dominated by grasses, sedges, and reeds. Both are species-rich habitats; indeed, fens can contain a huge diversity of wildlife and a staggering variety of plants. However fens are fast disappearing as the land is drained for agriculture, and because they are often areas where water collects, pollution can accumulate causing long term change. A lot of upland bog is quite degraded, most likely due to a combination of factors such as air pollution (particularly when coal was the main fuel), heavy grazing and frequent burning. Degraded bog often has a high cover of hare's-tail cotton-grass with little or no sphagnum moss; however, there are still pockets of sphagnum-rich bog here and there, some of which have been fenced off to prevent stock getting trapped.

Bog.

Fen.

Peat hags.

Blanket bog.

Raised bog.

Flushes.

Rhôs pasture.

Peat bog and marsh

Peat is a precious resource. Not only does it take thousands of years to form, but peat bogs are important habitats for a whole range of species. Sadly, many of the larger peat bogs in the UK have been overexploited by the commercial extraction of horticultural peat, and many more have been damaged by drainage, forestry and inappropriate management. Although peat is still forming in some bogs, the rate of formation is far less than the rate of loss. Not only is this leading to the destruction of a valuable habitat, but in some areas, it is also causing the underlying bedrock to become exposed, causing greater likelihood of flash flooding and erosion downstream.

Blanket bog

Blanket bogs are formed when large areas of level or gently sloping ground are smothered by a 'blanket' of peat. They are wild areas with spiky rushes, carpets of moss and wet, peaty soils, and they are a walker's nightmare! Although species-poor because of its acidity, blanket bog has considerable wildlife interest, and contains a variety of unusual plants and animals adapted to this specialised habitat. Sphagnum mosses (page 58) play an important role in the creation of peat by retaining water, providing essential nutrients and preventing the decay of dead plant material which eventually becomes peat.

Raised bog

These unique habitats are formed when an accumulation of peat causes the bog surface to rise above the water table. Although they are now very scarce in the UK, the wet, cool climate means that Wales has some of the best raised bogs left, such as at the Craig y Cilau NNR near Crickhowell, and on Mynydd Bach Trecastell above Usk Reservoir. At Traeth Mawr near the National Park Visitor Centre, small patches of raised bog form hummocks in among the fen, creating a mixed habitat that is quite unique.

Flushes

Flushes often occur around spring-lines, or where underground water reaches the surface and creates an area of saturated ground as opposed to a well-defined channel. In gritstone areas these flushes tend to be very acidic and quite species-poor, with tall rushes and carpets of sphagnum and star moss; on the ORS and limestone the flushes tend to be more varied and species-rich, less dominated by rushes, and more open with lots of sedges and species like butterwort.

Rhôs pasture

Also known as purple moor grass and rush pasture, this nutrient-poor grass-land can be found across the National Park, particularly along the upland edge. The habitat is valuable because it supports a wide range of plants species. However, the tough grasses that characterise rhôs pasture are not liked by sheep, so the habitat is under threat as hill farmers try to improve the grazing.

Bedstraw *(Galium)* *Briwydden*

Common marsh bedstraw *(Galium palustre)* *Briwydden y gors* and **fen bedstraw** *(Galium uliginosum)* *Briwydden y fign* are common in wet grassland and flushes and are difficult to tell apart. They are very thin, straggly plants with hairless, square stems and small bunches of tiny, four-petalled cream flowers. They grow to about 50cm, and often scramble through other plants. Marsh bedstraw feels smooth, and usually has whorls of four leaves; whereas fen bedstraw feels rough and usually has whorls of six leaves. See also the general description on page 114.

Bog asphodel *(Narthecium ossifragum)* *Llafn y bladur*

Locally abundant in bogs and the more acidic flushes, this stunning plant has distinctive sword-like leaves and dense spikes of bright yellow, star-like flowers with prominent woolly stamens. It grows to about 20cm in height and flowers in July and August. In autumn, most of the plant turns bright orange and the flowers are replaced by reddish, egg-shaped fruits. The Latin name means 'bone breaker', and it was once mistakenly believed that sheep grazing on the plant would develop brittle bones. It has been also used as a source of saffron and as a yellow hair dye.

Bedstraw in wimberry.

Bog asphodel.

Brooklime.

Butterwort. © Julie Bell.

Butterwort leaves.

Brooklime *(Veronica beccabunga)* **Llysiau Taliesin**

This fleshy, succulent plant is often seen along stream edges and where water trickles. It has spikes of very small blue (sometimes pink) flowers, with large, rounded leaves and thick, juicy stems. It blooms between May and September. It was used all over northern Europe as a salad plant and was believed to help prevent scurvy.

Butterwort *(Pinguicula vulgaris)* **Tafod y gors**

Also known as bog violet or marsh violet, this carnivorous plant is confined to calcareous flushes. It has single, funnel-shaped, purple-blue flowers (one per stem), which nod gently about 12cm above flat rosettes of bright yellow-green sticky, starfish-like leaves. Any insect landing on the leaf is trapped, and the leaf then curls around it and digests it. Although the plant is seldom used in modern herbal medicine, it was commonly used in Wales in the past as a purgative. It has also been used as a cough remedy, and was believed to be particularly effective against whooping cough.

Hare's tail cottongrass.

Unfertilised cottongrass flowers.

Cottongrass *(Eriophorium)* *Plu'r gweunydd*

Cottongrass is a common sight on the moors in the Park, and the fluffy white seed heads can be so dense that it looks as though there has been snowfall. It is actually a sedge rather than a grass (see page 103), with unremarkable green or brown flowers that only develop into the distinctive tufts after fertilisation. Walkers would do well to detour around large patches of cottongrass, because these indicate that the area is really wet! There are two common species: **Common cottongrass** (*Eriophorium angustifolium*) *Plu'r gweunydd*, which has multiple, usually drooping spikes on short stems; and **Hare's tail cottongrass** (*Eriophorium vaginatum*) *Plu'r gweunydd unben*, which grows in tussocks and has a single spike on top of each long stem. Both grow up to 45cm high. Although the hairs are too brittle to spin into thread, they have been used to make candle wicks and paper, and the leaves and stems can be woven. The seeds and leaves are edible and are used in herbal medicine to treat diarrhoea and ailments of the gastrointestinal tract, and the stem contains pith which has been used to get rid of tapeworm.

Cowberry *(Vaccinium vitis-idaea)* *Llus goch*

Found in wet heath, particularly in the east of the Park, this low-creeping evergreen shrub has shiny oval leaves and white or pink bell-shaped flowers that develop into red berries. A relative of the wimberry (see page 128), its berries have such a sharp taste they are barely edible, but they are traditionally used to make a sauce for eating with game. Known as 'lingonberry' in Sweden and 'mountain cranberry' in North America, the plant is valued by herbalists who use it to treat a wide variety of ailments.

Cross-leaved heath *(Erica tetralix) Grug croesddail*

The most common heather in wet areas, cross-leaved heath is evergreen and has distinctive clusters of pink, bell-shaped flowers at the end of long, branched stems, which are covered with whorls of four leaves. It is usually the earliest heather to flower (from early July to September) and attracts many nectar-loving insects.

Crowfoot *(Ranunculus peltatus) Crafanc y frân y llyn*

There are many different types of crowfoot, and even the experts find identification tricky. They are basically white-flowered water-buttercups. Most have small, white, starry flowers and two types of leaves: surface leaves, which are generally three-lobed and broad, and underwater leaves, which are generally finely divided and feathery. You can find them in ponds, ditches and even wet mud, and they are often found in flushes.

Cowberry. © Colin Richards

Cross-leaved heath.

Crowfoot (and right and inset).

Cuckoo flower *(Cardamine pratensis)* **Bloddyn llefrith**

Cuckoo flower, also known as lady's-smock, is the county flower of Brecknockshire. It grows in damp, grassy places like wet meadows, as well as ditches, marshes, riverbanks and pond margins. It has a basal rosette of narrow leaves and an upright blue-green stem that carries one or sometimes two pale pink or lilac flowers, 1–2cm across, each with four petals. The arrival of the flowers is supposed to coincide with the arrival of the first cuckoo. The young leaves have a peppery taste and can be used in sandwiches and salads. However, picking cuckoo flower was considered unlucky, which may explain why the plant was rarely used in traditional medicine.

Devil's-bit scabious *(Succisa pratensis)* **Tamaid y cythraul**

Frequent in unimproved damp grassland along the upland edge and sometimes on damp ledges on upland crags, the rounded, nodding, dark-lilac flower heads of devil's-bit scabious can be found between July and October. Its round flower heads attract a wide variety of bees and butter-flies, including the exceptionally rare marsh fritillary. It has many medicinal properties, and legend has it that these angered the Devil so much that he tried to get rid of it by biting off its roots ... which are very short!

Golden Saxifrage *(Chrysosplenium oppositifolium)* **Tormaen**

Golden saxifrage is a moisture-loving creeping plant that forms mats of golden-green flowers. There are two species. **Opposite-leaved golden saxifrage** is the more common and can dominate damp banks in wood-land where it is one of the earlier species to flower. It has pairs of rounded, green leaves with small, golden flowers set among them. **Alternate-leaved golden saxifrage** *(Chrysosplenium alternifolium)* / *Eglyn Cylchddail* looks almost identical except that it is not quite so compact, and the leaves alternate along the flowering stem and do not grow in pairs.

Cuckoo flower.

Devil's bit scabious. © Anne Griffiths.

Opposite-leaved golden saxifrage. © Julie Bell.

Common-spotted orchid.

Common-spotted orchid (*Dactylorhiza fuchsii***)** *Tegeirian brych*
and Heath-spotted orchid *(Dactylorhiza maculata) Tegeirian*
brych y rhos

These two orchids are very similar and are often confused. The **common-spotted orchid** grows up to 50cm tall and prefers calcareous soils, whereas the **heath-spotted orchid** is rarely taller than about 20cm, has paler, more rounded flowers and narrower leaves, and prefers acid soils. Both have leaves that are marked with circular spots. They are commonly found in wet grassland along the upland edge but are rare on the open hill.

Lousewort *(Pedicularis sylvatica)* **Melog y cŵn**

Also known as dwarf red rattle, this very short (less than 2cm) plant is found in damp acid grassland but grows so low to the ground that it is easy to overlook. It has a mass of unbranched stems with tiny spikes of pale pink flowers and fern-like leaves, and if you see one, closer inspection often reveals several others in the same area. Its name comes from the mistaken belief that it gave lice to livestock grazing on it, whereas it actually provides a home for snails which carry the liver-fluke larvae.

Marsh marigold *(Caltha palustris)* **Gold y gors**

Also known as mayflower and kingcup, this is common in wet places. It has large, dark-green, waxy, kidney-shaped leaves, hollow stems, and golden-yellow flowers between 2cm and 5cm in diameter. Although the flowers usually have five petals, they can have up to nine. Like other members of the buttercup family, all parts of this plant are poisonous when fresh and have been known to cause skin irritation and dermatitis.

Lousewort. © Julie Bell.

Marsh marigold. © Anne Griffiths.

Meadowsweet.

Ragged Robin. © Julie Bell.

Roseroot. © Graham Motley.

Meadowsweet *(Filipendula ulmaria)* *Brenhines y Weirglodd*

The fluffy cream flower heads of meadowsweet can often be seen clustered together on top of long stems, and although you're unlikely to find this flower on peaty or acidic soils, it can be abundant in wet fields and flushes in limestone areas. It flowers from June to September, has a delicate aniseed fragrance in full sun, and its feathery leaves are sometimes covered with bright orange rust fungus. The flower heads are rich in salicylic acid, and the plant was traditionally used as a hangover remedy.

Ragged Robin *(Lychnis flos-cuculi)* *Carpiog y gors*

With bubble-gum-pink flowers, rough, narrow grass-like leaves and hairy stems up to 80cm tall, ragged robin is a delightful sight on a warm spring day in marshy grassland and flushes. An important source of nectar for butterflies and bees, the 3–4cm flowers have five petals, each deeply divided into four 'ragged' lobes. The roots are a source of saponin, a soapy substance that has been used as a shampoo. Although relatively harmless to humans, saponin is toxic to some creatures, and has been used by poachers to stun fish in brooks and small ponds.

Roseroot *(Sedum rosea)* *Pren y ddannoedd*

Common in neutral or calcareous flushes, roseroot is a succulent plant with waxy, grey-green leaves that spiral around a sturdy stem up to 30cm high. The fuzzy-looking greenish-yellow flowers form a cluster at the top of the stem, and the inner flowers turn red then brown with age. Sheep seem to love it, so it only grows where they can't get at it. If cut, the root smells of roses (hence its name) and it is still used in potpourri. It has been used in traditional European folk medicine for over 3,000 years and is believed to increase longevity and promote resistance to stress, fatigue and depression.

Sundew. Right: sundews and butterwort. © Julie Bell.

Sundew *(Drosera rotundifolia)* Gwlithlys

There are two species of sundew in the Park, the most common being **round-leaved sundew**. A low-growing, hairy plant often found among soggy mosses, it has small white flowers on a stalk up to 20cm tall. However, it is the leaves that make it interesting, for each leaf is covered in red 'hairs', each of which is tipped with a glistening droplet of sticky liquid. The twinkling droplets attract passing insects which get trapped in the sticky hairs, whereupon the leaf curls around the prey and digests it. Although much less common, you may also come across **oblong-leaved sundew** *(Drosera intermedia) (Gwlithlys hirddail)*, which has long, narrow leaves that taper abruptly to a long stalk.

Water avens *(Geum rivale)* Mapgoli glan y dŵr

Despite its name, this is not an aquatic plant, but a plant of damp places. It has nodding, multi-coloured, bell-shaped flowers which droop on a long purple stem up to 60cm high, with round leaves at its base. The flowers are followed by attractive, feathery, bur-like seed heads with reddish-brown hooks. Also known as 'chocolate root', the root is aromatic and has been used in the brewing industry and as a substitute for cocoa. It is used in herbal medicine as a tonic and an astringent, and is believed to have been used against the plague in the Middle Ages. The dried roots are traditionally used to repel moths.

Water avens. © Graham Motley.

Water mint *(Menthe aquatic) Mintys y dŵr*

Common in flushes and marshy grassland, water mint has hairy, oval leaves in whorls around reddish stems, and dense clusters of lilac-pink flowers from July to October. It spreads vigorously using creeping runners and grows to about 30cm tall. You'll know if you tread on it as the fragrance is unmistakeable! An important aromatic herb, herbalists prescribe it to treat headaches, indigestion and insomnia, and a tea made from its leaves is said to have a calming effect. However, Nicholas Culpeper wrote that mint 'stirs up bodily lust', and the Greeks warned their soldiers to avoid it in case their increased love-making affected their strength in battle.

Water mint.

Whorled caraway leaves.

Yellow iris.

Whorled caraway *(Carum verticillatum)* **Carwy droellenog**

Although very rare to the east of the A470, whorled caraway is a signature plant of the rhôs pastures in the west of the Park and is the county flower of Carmarthenshire. With frothy white blossoms in July and August, it initially looks like cow parsley, but closer inspection reveals a distinctive circlet or 'whorl' of leaves around the base of its stem. It is related to the **spice caraway** *(Carum carvi) Carwe sbeis* but has no culinary or medicinal use.

Yellow iris *(Iris pseudacorus)* **Gellhesg**

Also known as 'yellow flag', this tall (1–1.5 metre) plant has branched stems with long, sword-shaped leaves, and large, bright yellow flowers. Although mainly a lowland species, it can sometimes be found along the margins of upland streams and ponds. It is used in traditional medicine as an astringent, to stop blood flow, and is believed to have been the inspiration for the fleur-de-lis symbol which is used by the scouts. Its thick rhizome has been used to produce a black dye, and the roasted seeds can be used to make a drink that is said to resemble coffee.

Woodland and hedgerow

Woodland is the most common truly natural habitat in the National Park, and much of the native deciduous woodland is a meagre remnant of the much larger forest that grew here hundreds of years ago (see also Trees and shrubs – page 155). About 13% of the National Park is covered by trees, providing a rich habitat supporting a wide variety of plants. In addition to deciduous woodland, there are also large areas of coniferous plantation, often on land considered unproductive for other types of farming. Although these tend to create an environment disliked by many plants, they often contain many species of moss and fungi.

Depending on how hard the winter has been, the deciduous woods begin to spring to life towards the end of February. Catkins of all different shapes and sizes appear, and blocks of woodland begin to take on colour as the trees start to bud. Particularly noticeable is the purple hue of the birch woods when viewed from a distance.

Hedgerows were created to mark boundaries and to prevent stock from wandering. This created a new habitat that mimicked the native woodlands, especially as native trees were often used in their creation. There are over 5,500km of hedgerows in the National Park, so this is a significant upland edge habitat. Particularly in the east of the Park, where many hedgerows are believed to be remnants of the original forest, they support plants more typical of ancient woodland. Indeed, the variety of species in the older hedgerows can be staggering – the base of the hedge providing cover for woodland plants, while grassland species have moved from the

The purple hue of a birch wood.

Hedgerows.

surrounding fields to thrive under its protection. From mid-spring until late summer, the hedgerows are a riot of colour as plants compete for sunlight. Particularly notable are the blackthorns and hawthorns, which often have masses of blossom. They are easy to tell apart – the blackthorn comes into flower before the leaves appear (and is the earlier of the two); the hawthorn comes into leaf before the flowers appear (see also page 158). Hedgerows are also important as they create corridors that allow species to move between isolated blocks of woodland, and provide navigation landmarks, particularly for bats.

Hawthorn leaves.

Hawthorn flowers.

Blackthorn leaves.

Blackthorn flowers.

Native bluebell.

Bluebells (and white bells!).

Bluebell *(Hyacinthoides non-scripta)* *Clychau'r gog*

One of the nation's best-loved wild flowers, this needs no introduction. Sweetly scented, the usually blue flowers are sometimes white and occasionally pink. Almost half the world's population of bluebells grow in the UK, providing an early source of food for bees, hoverflies, butterflies and other insects. Bees sometimes bite a hole in the bottom of the bell, effectively 'stealing' the nectar without pollinating the flower. Bluebell sap has been used to bind pages into the spines of books, and our Bronze Age ancestors used it to stick feathers to their arrows. However, the sap can also cause contact dermatitis, and all parts of the plant are poisonous. According to folklore, fairies used bluebells to lure people walking through the woods, and anyone who hears a bluebell ring will soon die.

Although apparently common, the humble bluebell is actually under threat, because almost 20% of bluebells found in broadleaved woodland are the Spanish rather than the native species. The easiest way to tell the difference is to look at the pollen: native bluebells have creamy-white pollen; Spanish bluebells have blue or green pollen. Additionally, Spanish bluebells have little if any scent.

Common Cleavers *(Galium aparine)* *Gwlydd y perthi*

Also known as goosegrass, kisses, sticky bobs, sticky-Willy, sweethearts and Robin-run-the-hedge, this common scrambler sprawls across the ground and over other plants forming a dense network of stems and leaves up to 1.5 metres high. Common in hedgerows and along wooded upland edges, it has tiny white flowers from May to September. The leaves are arranged around the stems in whorls of 6 to 8, and both stems and leaves have minute hooks which help the plant to cling and climb – and to stick to your clothing if you brush past. The seeds can be roasted and used as a coffee substitute, and an infusion of cleavers is said to be extremely tasty with a hint of nuts. See also the general description of bedstraws on page 114.

Cuckoo-pint *(Arum maculatum)* *Pidyn y gog*

Also known as lords and ladies, cuckoo-pint is common along hedgerows and in ancient woodland. It first emerges from the ground in January as a narrow green spike that slowly unfurls to reveal a purple flower that resembles a fireworks sparkler, surrounded by a purple spotted leafy hood. By mid-summer, the flower is replaced by a cluster of green berries that turn bright red as the leaf decays, and these berry-laden stems last well into winter. Although the roasted roots can be used to produce a beverage, without proper preparation this can be toxic, so its use for casual refreshment is not advised! The berries are particularly poisonous, but all parts of the plant contain microscopic needle-shaped crystals which severely irritate the skin and can cause allergic reactions including stomach irritation, a swollen throat and breathing difficulties.

Dog's mercury *(Mercurialis perennis)* *Bresych y cŵn*

This widespread creeping plant can carpet ash woodland and shady banks so extensively that it pushes out everything else. It likes alkaline soils so can also be found on limestone pavements. It has hairy, toothed, spear-shaped, dark leaves on upright stems, with clusters of small, yellowish green flowers at the base of the leaves. It is not a pleasant plant (its scent has been compared to that of rotting fish, and it is poisonous) although small mammals and birds will eat its seeds if desperate. The leaves were once used to make a dye.

Common Cleavers.

Cuckoo-pint and (inset) berries.

Dog's mercury. © Graham Motley.

Early purple orchid.

Early-purple orchid *(Orchis mascula) Tegeirian coch y gwanwyn*

Often coming into flower at the same time as bluebells, this orchid thrives on limestone soils and can be found in a variety of habitats. Although not common, it is obvious when seen. It has a dense, cone-shaped cluster of pinkish-purple flowers on a spike that can grow to 50cm high, and narrow, glossy, dark green, spotted leaves which can appear as a rosette as early as January. It is delightfully fragrant when it first blooms, but this rapidly deteriorates into an unpleasant stench! These orchids have been widely used as an aphrodisiac, and the dried roots are used to make *salep* – a nutritious drink that was valued by manual workers during the 19th century.

Foxglove *(Digitalis purpurea)* **Bysedd y cŵn**

This very common and easily recognised plant has flower spikes up to two metres high with up to eighty bell-shaped blooms, usually purply-pink but occasionally white. The leaf base appears long before the flower, which can cause confusion. An excellent source of nectar and pollen for all kinds of insects, the plant is extremely poisonous and has the potential to kill in quite small amounts ... yet it is also the source of a medicine that has saved thousands of lives. In folklore, foxgloves are fairy houses, and the mottled markings on the petals were said to be fairy handprints. Children were told it was bad luck to disturb the plant as this would lead to the fairies being homeless and bad-tempered.

Herb Bennet *(Geum urbanum)* **Mapgoll**

Also known as wood avens, this hairy, erect plant is a common sight in old deciduous woodland and hedgerows from May to August. It has downy triple-lobed leaves and loose clusters of five-petalled flowers; the seed heads resemble burrs and have tiny red hooks that cling to anything that brushes past. The plant has a long history of medicinal use, and the root has a distinct flavour of cloves. It was used instead of hops in medieval ales and is still used to flavour Benedictine liqueur. It can also be used as a replacement for cloves in spicy recipes.

Herb Robert *(Geranium robertianum)* **Y Goesgoch**

This short to medium hairy plant has a strong smell, and is common in moist, shady places. The flowers have five round-ended, bright pink petals, 14–18mm across. The leaves have 3–5 lobes, and the reddish branching stems are fairly fragile. It has many local names including granny-thread-the-needle, stinking Robert, and pink pinafores. In folklore it is said to be the plant of the house goblin, and in homeopathy, the plant is used to treat internal bleeding. The fresh leaves are edible and can be used in salads, while the dried leaves can be used to make an antiseptic infusion to clean wounds, treat skin eruptions, and relieve mouth and gum infections. Rubbing fresh leaves on the skin is said to repel mosquitoes.

Lesser celandine *(Ficaria verna)* *Llygad Ebrill*

These yellow star-like flowers are one of the earliest signs of spring, often carpeting woodland with a splash of colour and providing insects with an important food source. The glossy, dark green, heart-shaped leaves have long stems, and the shiny yellow flowers have 8–12 petals. It was once believed that the flowers could be used to predict the weather as they close their petals a short time before it starts to rain. The plant is rich in vitamin C, and was once used to prevent scurvy. Herbalists also use it as a remedy for haemorrhoids – hence its alternative name: pilewort.

Foxglove leaves.

Foxglove.

Herb Bennet. © Graham Motley.

Herb Bennet flower.

Herb Robert.

Lesser celandine.

Primrose *(Primula vulgaris)* **Briallu**

The humble primrose, awarded the accolade of Wales' favourite flower in 2015, is another plant that needs no introduction. It prefers woodland clearings and hedgerows, but is hardy enough to be found virtually anywhere, and will even flower in January if the weather is mild. Wild primroses often grow in clusters, and usually have large, creamy flowers with deeper yellow centres, although they can be any shade from white to dark yellow – even in the same cluster. According to tradition, if you plant a primrose upside-down, the flower will be red; in folk medicine, primroses were considered to be a powerful treatment for rheumatism and gout. The flowers are edible and were once popular in an Easter dish known as primrose pottage. They can also be infused to make primrose tea.

Ramsons *(Allium ursinum)* **Craf y geifr**

More commonly known as wild garlic, this plant is unmistakeable as it gives off a distinctive smell of garlic. Indeed, you can often smell it before you see it. It loves ancient deciduous woodland (particularly ash woodland), and often forms grey-green carpets of long, pointed, oval leaves, with clusters of small, white, six-petalled flowers on a long, straight, leafless stems. The leaves are edible and sought after by foragers, but care is needed as they resemble the dangerously poisonous leaves of lily-of-the-valley, so they are best gathered individually rather than in handfuls. The bulbs are used in traditional medicine to lower cholesterol, and to treat a wide range of conditions including rheumatism and hypertension.

Red campion *(Silene dioica)* **Blodyn taranau**

Common on hedge banks and along the wooded upland edge, red campion has hairy leaves and stems, and rose-red flowers with five deeply notched petals. It usually flowers in May, just as the bluebells finish, and they can sometimes grow side-by-side for a few days, turning a woodland floor into a riot of pink and blue. Red campion seeds were once used in traditional medicine to treat snakebites.

Primrose.

Ramsons.

Red campion.

Snowdrops.

Snowdrop *(Galanthus nivalis)* *Eirlys*

There over 2,000 varieties of snowdrop, and although not a native species they are now well-established in the wild, thriving in lightly shaded woodland. The plants have two linear leaves and a single small white drooping bell-shaped flower with six petal-like tepals in two circles. The smaller inner petals have green markings. In British folklore, snowdrops symbolise purity and hope. The plant contains a substance called galantamine, which is used in the treatment of Alzheimer's disease. However, the bulbs themselves are poisonous, and there is a superstition that a single snowdrop bloom in a house represents death.

Stitchwort *(Stellaria)*

You will find the pretty star-shaped flowers of stitchwort growing in woods and hedgerows, taking over as one of the more common white flowers as the snowdrops fade. **Greater stitchwort** *(Stellaria holostea) Serenllys mawr* has 2–3cm wide flowers, while **lesser stitchwort** *(Stellaria graminea) Serenllys bach* has smaller flowers (0.5–1cm across). Although the flowers in both species have five white petals, these are so deeply notched that it looks as if the flowers have ten petals. The plants have many other names including star-of-Bethlehem and poor-man's button-hole. They are also sometimes called snapdragon because the brittle stems break easily, and popgun because the seeds explode when ripe. The name stitchwort comes from the belief that the plant can be used to prevent stitches caused by exercise.

Toothwort *(Lathraea squamaria) Deintlys*

This parasitic plant lives on hazel, alder or elm, and likes deep shade. Although difficult to see, it can often be found at the Pwll-y-Wrach and Coed y Cerrig Nature Reserves in the eastern part of the Park and is usually at its peak in April. It has white, downy stems and creamy-pink, tubular flowers which grow along one side of a spike up to about 25cm high. The small, white leaves look more like scales than leaves. The plant was once known as corpse flower because it was believed that it would grow from the ground above a buried body.

Wood anemone *(Anemone nemorosa) Blodyn y gwynt*

One of the earliest spring flowers, and particularly abundant in ash woodlands, wood anemone is a low-growing plant with solitary star-like white or purple-streaked flowers with 5–8 large petals, often pinkish underneath, deeply lobed leaves and a thin, red stem. Also known as windflower and grandma's nightcap, it has a distinctive sharp, musky smell. Hoverflies are particularly fond of this plant and help pollinate it, but other animals will only eat it if nothing else is available, and it is poisonous to humans.

Stitchwort.

Toothwort. © Anne Griffiths.

Wood anemone.

Wood sorrel.

Wood sorrel *(Oxalia acetosella)* *Suran y coed*

Forming distinct clump-like cushions, wood sorrel has fresh green, tre-foil leaves with heart-shaped lobes, and delicate white flowers with five petals and tiny purple veins. It grows in shady hedgerows and woodland (particularly oak woodland), often emerging from moss covered logs, and can sometimes be found in shaded spots on hillsides, where it indicates that the area was once wooded. The flowers and leaves both close as night falls and re-open at sunrise the next morning. All parts of the plant are edible, with a citrus kick that resembles lemon and apple peel – a real thirst-quencher on a hot day. However, they also contain oxalic acid, so should not be eaten in large quantities.

Ash tree; (top inset) leaves and (bottom inset) buds.

TREES AND SHRUBS

Three thousand years ago, much of the Brecon Beacons area was covered in trees. This ancient forest covered most of the valleys, but probably did not extend above about 650 metres, so it is unlikely that the highest peaks have ever been tree covered. This original woodland would have been a mixture of oak, ash and birch, with smaller species such as hawthorn, holly and hazel growing beneath the canopy and dense stands of alder in the wetter valley bottoms. Although the original woodlands have been largely cleared, remnants can still be seen on the rockier slopes and in the deeper, steeper gullies, where there have probably been trees for hundreds of years.

In addition to the native deciduous woodlands, there are large areas of commercial forestry dominated by unnatural straight ranks of fast-growing softwoods such as spruce, larch and pine (see also page 244). These dark forests may appear sterile, but they contain many species of moss and fungi, and several birds of prey make their nests in tall conifers. They also provide shelter for a wide range of small insects, which in turn provide a vital food source for several species of bat.

A few of the trees you are most likely to see on the uplands and the upland edge are described below.

Ash *(Fraxinus excelsior)* **Onnen**

The third most common native British tree (after oak and birch), ash trees can live to be over 400 years old. They have pale 'ash' coloured bark which cracks as the tree gets older, and compound leaves comprising 3–6 opposing pairs of light-green leaflets with a single leaflet at the end. These leaves move to capture the light, and sometimes the whole crown of the tree will lean towards the sun. In autumn, the leaves fall while they are still green, and in winter the smooth twigs have upturned ends and distinctive black, velvety leaf buds. Ash likes deep, well-drained limestone soils, but is a vigorous pioneer and will happily spread into upland areas given half a chance. Indeed, the upland ash woods in the south-west of the Park are some of the finest in Britain. Ash trees were thought to have mystical and medicinal properties and the wood was burned to ward off evil spirits. Newborn babies were often given a teaspoon of ash sap, and sick children were passed naked through a specially cut cleft in an ash tree, the cleft being bound after the ceremony to heal with the child. In Celtic literature, the ash tree is associated with the Welsh Magician-God, Gwyddion, who carries an ash staff. Widely coppiced, the wood was once used to make charcoal, furniture and tool handles.

The purple hue of a birchwood.

Birch.

Birch catkins (male).

Birch *(Betula pubescens)* *Bedwen*

Rarely more than 80 years old, birch (aka downy birch) is a pioneering species that quickly colonises disturbed ground. One of the two most common native British tree species (the other being the oak) birches were among the first trees to appear in Britain after the last Ice Age. The leaves are rounded triangles with toothed edges and a well-defined central stalk, and the bark (which makes excellent kindling for a campfire) is reddish in young trees, becoming greyer as the trees matures, eventually developing dark, horizontal streaks or 'lenticels'. In late spring, both male and female catkins are found on the same tree – the male catkins are long, yellow and droopy, and hang in small groups from the ends of shoots; the short, bright green, erect female catkins turn crimson and thicken after pollination. In folklore, witches' broomsticks were made from birch twigs treated with fly agaric mushrooms, and the twigs were also used to drive out evil spirits – the origin of 'beating the bounds' ceremonies. In Welsh mythology, birch trees symbolise renewal, and herbalists use birch leaves to treat cystitis and other urinary tract infections, to dissolve kidney stones and relieve rheumatism and gout. The sweet sap is used to make a wonderful country wine.

Blackthorn *(Prunus spinose)* *Draenen ddu*

Blackthorn is often confused with hawthorn (see below), but there is an easy way to tell them apart: blackthorn flowers appear before its leaves; hawthorn leaves appear before its flowers. Masses of white blackthorn flowers appear in March or April, often in a cold period following a false spring. Such cold snaps are traditionally known as 'blackthorn winters'. Widely occurring in hedgerows, the plant has small, oval leaves and five-petalled flowers. In autumn and winter, it produces bitter blue-black 'sloes' with a whitish bloom, used to make sloe gin. Blackthorn has a sinister reputation in Celtic folklore, and often represents the dark side of witchcraft. However, although associated with bad luck, it is also linked to the overcoming of negativity and the transformation that struggle can bring. Known as 'straif' by the Celts, this name is believed to be the origin of the word 'strife'.

Dwarf willow *(Salix herbacea)* *Helygen fach*

This tiny creeping plant is one of the smallest woody plants in the world – so small, in fact, that you can walk across it without even noticing it's there. Well adapted to living in harsh sub-arctic environments, you will only find it above about 650 metres, where it often grows as ground cover. There are many on the summit of Pen Cerrig-calch in the Black Mountains, where it rarely grows to more than 3cm in height. It has round, shiny leaves about 1.5cm in diameter.

Blackthorn leaves.

Blackthorn flowers.

Sloes.

Dwarf willow.

Hawthorn *(Crataegus monogyna)* **Draenen wen**

Hawthorn comes into leaf in April, then bursts into bloom in May – hence is folk name: mayflower. Like blackthorn, the plant is very thorny, with densely branched, dark brown stems; unlike blackthorn, the leaves are deeply lobed, and the flat-topped clusters of five-petalled flowers are highly scented. While the flowers are usually white, in some years they can be pink. The young leaves and flowers are edible and are traditionally known as 'bread and cheese', and they were once commonly added to salads together with the flower buds, which some people considered a delicacy. The flowers eventually produce dark red berries (haws), which although unpleasant if eaten raw, are used in traditional ketchups and jellies. In Medieval times it was thought that hawthorn blossom smelled like the Great Plague and bringing it into a house would result in illness and death. More recently it has been discovered that the blossoms contain trimethylamine, which is one of the first chemicals formed in decaying animal tissue. Also known as 'fairy trees', hawthorns were believed to have magical properties and were often left uncut, even when hedges were being removed. However, sheep do not have such inhibitions, and hawthorn bushes are often prevented from developing into larger trees by the grazing action of sheep.

Hazel *(Corylus avellana)* **Collen**

Hazel is a small shrubby tree with shiny, brown bark (which peels with age) and almost circular, toothed leaves with soft hairs on the underside. The young shoots are so bendy that they can be tied in a knot without breaking. The male yellow catkins appear in spring, alongside tiny, bud-like, red female flowers. The nuts appear in late summer, although most are eaten by small mammals before they fully ripen. Although it can reach a height of 12m, it is often coppiced, and although this stunts its growth, it extends its life from about 80 years to several hundred years. In Welsh folklore, the hazel was another fairy tree and was often planted near holy wells. Hazel twigs were used for water divining, and thicker rods for pilgrims' staffs and shepherds' crooks. One of the sacred trees of Celtic folklore, hazel nuts were believed to engender wisdom and creative inspiration.

Hawthorn flowers and (right) leaves.

Haws.

Sheep-cropped hawthorn.

Hazel.

Hazel nuts.

Holly (and right).

Holly *(Ilex aquifolium) Celynnen*

Another of the sacred trees of Celtic mythology, it is still considered unlucky to cut down a holly. It is regarded as the evergreen twin of the oak, and while the oak is said to control the lighter half of the year, the holly controls the darker months. Up to 15m high and 300 years old, hollies have smooth, thin bark with numerous small, brown 'warts', dark brown stems, and dark green, glossy, oval leaves. The spiky leaves are characteristic of younger plants, but the leaves of older trees are much more likely to be smooth, as are leaves in the upper parts of the tree. The white, four-petalled flowers develop into distinctive scarlet berries which can remain on the tree throughout winter. Druids believed the holly symbolised peace and goodwill, and that it would guard against witches, goblins and the devil. Bringing holly leaves inside over winter provided shelter for fairies who, in turn, would be kind and helpful. Newborn babies were once protected from harm by being bathed in the water from the leaves. The wood is the whitest of all woods and is much prized for furniture making and engraving. It is heavy, hard and fine grained, can be stained and polished, and is often used to make walking sticks.

Sessile oak.

Pedunculate oak (and below).

Oak *(Quercus) Derwen*

Two species of oak are seen in the Park – **sessile oak** *(Quercus petraea)*
Derwen ddigoe and **pedunculate oak** *(Quercus robur) Derwen goesog*.
Sessile oak is the more common and represents remnants of the original
forest, whereas pedunculate oak prefers richer soils so has been largely
cleared to make space for farmland. You can easily tell them apart: sessile
oak has a 1–2cm leaf stalk whereas pedunculate oak has a leaf stalk of
less than 5mm. Oak has always been a sacred tree representing strength
and truth, and it was once thought that fairies lived in oak trees during the
summer months. There is also a long-standing connection with druids who
thought a tree especially sacred if it contained mistletoe, and the name 'druid'
means 'oak wisdom'. Acorns are not produced until a tree is at least 40 years
old, and acorn production peaks in trees aged between 80–120 years. It was
once believed that carrying an acorn guarded against disease and promoted
longevity, planting an acorn during a new moon would bring wealth, and an
acorn placed in a window would protect a house from lightning.

Rowan *(Sorbus aucuparia)* *Cerddinen*

Rowan is also known as mountain ash, probably due to the fact that it grows at a higher altitude than any other tree in the country and its grey-green feathery leaves are similar to those of ash, even though the two species are not related. It is a small but strong deciduous tree, which can grow to 7m even in poor soil. It has clusters of 5–10mm five-petalled white flowers in May, and orange or red berries appear in late summer every three or four years. These berries have a five-pointed star on the end furthest from the stalk – a pentagram shape that was believed to be a symbol of protection. Indeed, rowan trees were widely planted close to houses as a protection against witches, and in graveyards to protect the spirits of the dead. Rowan wood was used in pocket charms to guard against rheumatism, and to make divining rods, walking sticks and spinning wheels, and rowan spoons were used for stirring milk to prevent it curdling.

Rowan berries are full of vitamin C, and although edible, are unpleasantly sour. They were once used in the treatment of scurvy and to make a tonic, and they are still used to make a traditional cough syrup. Rowan berry jelly is particularly good with goose.

Rowan with berries (unripe).

Rowan sapling.

Rowan with berries (ripe).

Silver birch.

Silver birch *(Betula pendula)* *Bedwen arian*

Silver birch is a vigorous, light-demanding pioneer which quickly occupies bare ground. Reaching heights of up to 30m, it can be distinguished from downy birch (see above) by its drooping branch tips and the dark, diamond-shaped fissures in the white, paper-like bark, which can be easily peeled in thin sheets. Additionally, young twigs are hairless and covered with warts, whereas those of downy birch are hairy but smooth. As the tree matures, it sheds layers of bark to the extent that the base becomes dark and rugged. The wood is not much used in the UK as the trees rarely grow big enough, but the best *vihtas* (the whisks used in saunas) are made from the twigs. The leaves are used in herbal medicine and to make a refreshing tea, and the sap is used as a stimulating drink in spring.

Whitebeam.

Yew.

Whitebeams *(Sorbus) Cerdin*

Although usually uncommon in the wild, you will almost certainly see these shrubby trees if you visit the limestone areas in the south east of the Park, particularly around the spectacular nature reserves at Darren Fawr near Merthyr Tydfil, and Craig y Cilau near Crickhowell, where several species survive. Most notable are **lesser whitebeam** *(Sorbus minima) Cerddinen wen fach*, **thin-leaved whitebeam** *(Sorbus leptophylla) Cerddinen Gymreig* and **Ley's whitebeam** *(Sorbus leyana) Cerddin y Darren Fach* – all of which are exceptionally rare. Indeed, in 2014 there were only 13 known specimens of Ley's whitebeam in the world, most of them clinging to steep limestone cliffs with their trunks pressed close to the rock face. Although they resemble rowans, whitebeams can be recognised by their oval leaves (which have whitish undersides that reflect the light – hence 'white-beam'), the clusters of white flowers that appear in late spring, and the bright red berries that appear in autumn.

Yew *(Taxus baccata)* *Ywen*

Although more common in the lowlands, yew trees occasionally grow on limestone crags. As a species, they are incredibly long lived, and there are many ancient yews in churchyards in the Park, the most famous being at St Cynog's church in Defynnog, believed to be 5,000 years old. The tree has a long association with folklore and was considered sacred by the Druids, to whom it symbolised death and resurrection. The foliage and berry casing are highly toxic, although the fleshy red part of the berries is loved by blackbirds who act as efficient seed dispersers, and a homoeopathic tincture made from young shoots and the berry flesh is used to treat neuralgia and cystitis. Yew needles also contain 'taxanes', which are effective in the treatment of certain cancers. The wood is very hard and close-grained, and although sought after in furniture making, is probably best known as the material from which medieval longbows were made.

Cherry laurel.

INVADERS

Below is a list of plants you will almost certainly see, but which should not really be here!

Cherry laurel *(Prunus laurocerasus)* *Coeden lawrgeirios*
A small to medium-sized evergreen tree up to about 10 metres tall, this has shiny dark green leaves that smell of almonds when crushed. The flower buds open in early summer to form long clusters of creamy-white, sweet-smelling flowers, which develop into cherry-like fruits in autumn. All parts of the plant are poisonous and may cause severe discomfort to humans if ingested. The seeds are poisonous, containing cyanogenic glycosides and amygdalin. Laurel water, made from the plant, contains prussic acid and other compounds and is toxic. The problems posed by cherry laurel are similar to those of rhododendron: its rapid growth and dense habit allow it to out-compete and kill off native species. Its leaves, which are said to ward off evil spirits, contain cyanide, making them unpalatable to livestock and other grazing animals.

Cotoneaster.

Cotoneaster *(Cotoneaster)*

These popular garden plants can be both deciduous and evergreen depending on the species and can grow as shrubs or small trees. They are characterised by clusters of small pink or white flowers in early summer, followed by red or purple berries in autumn. These berries are popular with birds which spread the seed; this is most likely how they spread to the mountains in the first place. Once in the wild, they are difficult to eradicate and they out-compete native species. They are especially problematic in limestone areas, particularly on cliffs, pavements and screes where many rare native species grow. The berries of some species have been used in traditional herbal medicine for the treatment of diarrhoea, and stomach and intestinal inflammation.

Giant hogweed.

Giant hogweed *(Heracleum mantegazzianum)* **Efwr enfawr**

Brought into Britain as an ornamental plant in Victorian times, this tall, cow parsley-like plant has thick bristly stems, large jagged leaves, and white flowers in heads that can be 60cm across. It can grow to a height of 3 metres. It likes damp places and is found alongside rivers and pond margins. It may look impressive, but its sap contains toxins that are activated by sunlight, and contact with the skin can cause blisters, severe allergic reactions and serious, recurring skin damage. Our native **hogweed** *(Heracleum sphondylium) Panasen y cawr* is a much smaller plant, growing to a height of just 2 metres, but it can also cause severe rashes and other skin complaints. The best thing to do if you see this plant is avoid it!

Himalayan balsam *(Impatiens glandulifera) Jac y neidiwr*

Another plant that was introduced by the Victorians, this plant soon became widely naturalised, especially close to towns. Growing up to 3 metres tall, it is reputed to be the UK's tallest annual plant. It is very fast-growing and spreads rapidly and densely, invading wet habitat at the expense of native flowers. When the plants die down in winter they leave large areas of bare ground that are sensitive to erosion. Its seed pods explode when touched, flinging the seeds distances of up to 7 metres. Each pod holds up to 16 waterproof seeds, which float down nearby rivers and thereby colonise new areas further downstream. The seeds are edible with a slightly peppery taste.

Himalayan balsam (and right).

Giant knotweed.

Rhododendron.

Spanish bluebell.

Knotweed *(Fallopia) Canclwm*

There are two species of knotweed here, mainly in damp areas along riverbanks and lake shores. Both have large, heart-shaped leaves, and produce dense spikes of small green-white flowers in summer. The more common is **Japanese knotweed** *(Fallopia japonica) Clymog Japan*, which can now be found all over the UK. It grows rapidly, producing incredibly strong, underground runners that can push through walls, paving, and even concrete. The runners eventually clog the soil, while the shoots form such a dense canopy that it becomes too dark for anything else to grow. The much larger **giant knotweed** *(Fallopia sachalinensis) Y glymog fawr* can grow up to 5 metres high in a single season. It has large leaves and forms dense thickets. It can also hybridise with Japanese knotweed to give a highly invasive hybrid species. The hollow stems can be used to make flutes, and the fresh young shoots are edible, with a delicious earthy tartness that is versatile and distinctive. In terms of taste and texture, it lies somewhere between rhubarb and asparagus, which means it can be used in both desserts and savoury dishes.

Common rhododendron *(Rhododendron ponticum)* **Rhododendron wyllt**

First introduced to the UK from Spain in the 18th century, this attractive plant has spread widely and readily naturalises, particularly in wooded areas, open habitats on acid soils, and areas with naturally high humidity. Although usually a shrub, it can also grow into a small tree given time, and once established it is notoriously difficult to eradicate as it spreads rapidly by both seeds and suckers and cut limbs will re-root if left on the ground. It may look pretty, but its dense foliage creates too much shade for our native ground flora, and it even produces chemicals that suppress the growth of seedlings and native shrubs ... an effect that continues long after the rhododendron has been removed. These chemicals also mean that the spread of the plant cannot be controlled by grazing as it is toxic to sheep and cattle. It is also toxic to humans, and honey made from rhododendron flowers can cause short-term cardiac and intestinal problems known as 'mad honey disease'.

Spanish Bluebell *(Hyacinthoides hispanica)* **Clychau'r Gog Sbaenaidd**

See bluebells, page 145.

ANIMALS

The range of fauna in the region is just as extensive as that of the flora, and the variety of species is an important part of the area's biodiversity.

Common carder bee.

Heath bumblebee.

INSECTS / TRYCHFILOD

There are so many insects out there, it's difficult to know where to start! What follows is merely a tiny selection of some of the more common and is by no means representative. Indeed, I have not included any information about flies (of which there are hundreds) or ants (of which there are a few); nor about wasps, lacewings, earwigs, grasshoppers, and a whole host of other creepy crawlies. Those alone would fill an entire book! Think of this as a good start.

Bumblebee / Cacwn

Bees turn up everywhere, even in our everyday sayings: 'as busy as a bee'; 'make a bee-line'; and 'getting a bee in your bonnet'. The term 'bee's knees' is now used to refer to something excellent, although originally it meant something small and insignificant. In Wales it was once considered lucky if bees set up home near a house as they were believed to bless it with prosperity. In modern folk magic, bumblebees act as charms for health and wealth, and bee stings are used to treat rheumatism and arthritis.

There are currently 22 species of bumblebee found in Wales, including some important rarities. The list below includes four of the more commonly seen in the Brecon Beacons.

Common carder bee *(Bombus pascuorum) Gwenynen Gribob*

One of our most common bumblebees, the common carder bee is brown and orange, sometimes with darker bands on its abdomen. It can be seen from March to November. It nests in cavities, such as old mouse runs, and nests may contain up to 200 workers.

Heath bumblebee *(Bombus jonellus) Cacynen y rhos*

A common sight on heath land between March and early September, this small bumblebee has a white tail and three yellow bands – one at the front and two at the back. It nests in a variety of habitats including old bird nests, old mouse runs, and among moss and leaf litter. The nests are generally small with fewer than 50 workers.

Red-tailed bumblebee *(Bombus lapidarius) Cacynen dingoch*

The red-tailed bumblebee can be seen feeding on flowers from March until November. The black females are very large with a big red tail. Males are smaller and have two yellow bands on their thorax, and one at the base of their abdomen. The nest size varies considerably, some containing over 200 bees, while other have less than 100.

White-tailed bumblebee *(Bombus lucorum) Cacynen gynffonwen*

One of the first bees to emerge from hibernation, the white-tailed bumble-bee has black and lemon bands and a pure white tail. It is very common and can be seen right through to late November, wherever there are flow-ers. They nest in holes in the ground, often using old mouse or vole nests, and nests may contain as many as 400 workers.

Red-tailed bumblebee.

White-tailed bumblebee.

Dragonflies and damselflies / *Gwlyb y neidr a melinogion*

More than twenty species of dragonflies and damselflies can be seen in the National Park between May and October. Their larvae develop in clean water (both still and running), so lakes, ponds, streams, rivers, canals and bogs are good places to look for flying adults. The best time to see them is a couple of hours either side of noon on warm calm days.

Damselflies *(Zygoptera)* have a weak, fluttering flight. They close their wings when resting, and their eyes do not touch at the top of their head.

Dragonflies *(Anisoptera)* have a strong, purposeful flight. They hold their wings open when resting, and their eyes touch at the top of their head. Here are a few of the more common.

Black darter *(Sympetrum danae) Picellwr du*
Common darter *(Sympetrum striolatum) Picellwr cyffredin*
These small, narrow-bodied dragonflies are common on moorlands, heaths and bogs from the end of June until late October. The **black darter** is the only small dragonfly that is almost entirely black – males are black with dark yellow spots along the sides; females and juveniles are brownish-yellow. Male **common darters** are bright red; females and juveniles are golden-brown. They hover in a stationary position, then suddenly dart forward to catch their small insect prey which they then consume on a favourite perch.

Male black darter.
© Keith Noble.

Female black darter.
© Keith Noble.

Common darter.
© Keith Noble.

Broad-bodied chaser *(Libellula depressa)* **Picellwr boliog**

This medium-sized dragonfly is noticeably 'fat'. Common around pools from the end of May to August, it uses a perch in vegetation on the side of the pool as a base from which to make swift flights out over the water looking for insects. The male is powder-blue with yellow spots along its sides, and the female is greenish-brown.

Common blue damselfly *(Enallagma cyathigerum)* **Mursen las gyffredin**

There are seven species of small blue damselflies, of which this is the most common. The male is blue; the female is either blue or grey-green. Both have bands of black along their body. When common blues mate they form a 'mating wheel' in which the male clasps the female by the neck and she bends her body around in response.

Common hawker *(Aeshna juncea)* **Gwas-neidr glas**

This large dragonfly can be seen around upland pools from late June until October. The largest and fastest flying dragonflies, they can hover or fly backwards, and like all dragonflies they catch their prey in flight. Mostly black in colour, the male has dark-blue eyes and pale-blue spots and yellow flecks all along its body; the female has yellowish spots and brownish eyes.

Emerald damselfly *(Lestes sponsa)* **Mursen werdd**

The metallic-green, emerald damselfly is a medium-sized damselfly which can be distinguished from other damselflies by their habit of holding their wings half-open, rather than closed. The last species of damselfly to emerge each year, they can be seen from the end of June to September.

Four-spotted chaser *(Libellula quadrimaculata)* **Picellwr pedwar nod**

A medium-sized, broad-bodied dragonfly that can be seen around upland pools from early June to August, this is a very active dragonfly, spending much of the day hunting or marking out their territories. They are golden-brown with yellow spots along their sides, and have two distinctive dark spots at the front edge of each wing.

Golden-ringed dragonfly *(Cordulegaster boltonii)* *Gwas-neidr eurdorchog*

A common sight along rocky sections of upland streams from May to September, this very large dragonfly is a fast and powerful flyer. Black with yellow bands along the body and bright-green eyes, they are fierce predators, feeding on large insects such as damselflies, other dragonflies, wasps, beetles and bumblebees. The female is the UK's longest dragonfly and can be 8.5cm long.

Broad-bodied chaser. © Keith Noble.

Common blue damselfly.

Common hawker. © Keith Noble.

Emerald damselfly. © Keith Noble.

Four-spotted chaser. © Keith Noble.

Golden-ringed dragonfly. © Keith Noble.

Golden-ringed dragonfly just emerged from its larval state. © Julie Bell.

Butterflies / Gloÿnnod byw

In recent years approximately 30 species of butterfly have been recorded here, including the very rare marsh fritillary, which you are unlikely to see. The list below includes some of the species you are most likely to see in the uplands and along the upland edges.

Comma *(Polygonia c-album) Mantell Garpiog*

You can sometimes see these rich orangey-brown butterflies on the upland edge close to hill gates or handling pens, or anywhere where there are nettles. They have a distinctive ragged edge to their wings. Once in severe decline, they are now making a comeback, and are responding to climate change by moving to more northern habitats.

Common blue *(Polyommatus icarus) Glesyn cyffredin*

This butterfly can be seen in a variety of grassy habitats all over the Park, particularly in conjunction with common bird's-foot-trefoil (see page 115), its main foodplant. The male has blue wings with a black-brown border and a thin white fringe, while the female is brown with a blue dusting near its body and a few orange spots along the lower edges of its wings.

Grayling *(Hipparchia semele) Gweirlöyn llwyd*

Although not common and sadly in decline, this large, brown butterfly can sometimes be seen in summer in disused limestone quarries along the southern boundary of the Park. It is well-camouflaged when on the ground, but if you follow one in flight it usually soon settles with its wings held tightly together.

Green hairstreak *(Callophrys rubi) Brithribin gwyrdd*

The only green butterfly in the UK, the green hairstreak is aggressively territorial. Although the undersides of its wings are metallic green, the upper surface is brown. Look for it from late-April until mid-July on heather and bilberry moors and along the upland edge where there is hawthorn, rowan or gorse.

Comma.

Common blue. © Sarah Maliphant www.more-to.org

Grayling. © Graham Motley.

Green hairstreak. © Keith Noble.

Green-veined white.

Green-veined white *(Pieris napi) Gwyn gwythiennau gwyrddion*

This butterfly is widespread along the edges of upland commons and rhôs pasture, and most white butterflies in the uplands will be this species. It can be distinguished from other 'whites' by the green veins on the underside of its hind-wing. If you time it right, you may be lucky enough to see several hundred in the air at the same time as they emerge from their pupae.

Painted lady *(Vanessa cardui)* **Mantell Dramor**

This hill-topping migrant can be seen flying swiftly across the uplands in spring (heading north) and autumn (heading south). It has orange-brown wings with black and white spots on the forewing; the undersides are mottled brown with spots.

Red admiral *(Vanessa atalanta)* **Mantell goch**

Another hill topping migrant, large numbers of red admirals can be seen heading north in late-spring and south in autumn as they fly in a direct manner across even the highest hill-tops. They are easily recognised by their red and black wings with a white band near the tip of the fore-wing.

Ringlet *(Aphantopus hyperantus)* **Gweirlöyn y glaw**

A medium-sized, dark brown butterfly, often seen in rhôs pasture, its wings usually have a creamy edge, with several small pale spots underneath. It has a low, lazy flight, moving only short distances, then settling with open wings. Sometimes confused with the meadow brown, the latter is larger with an obvious single spot on each forewing.

Small heath *(Coenonympha pamphilus)* **Gweirlöyn bach y waun**

This small butterfly is predominantly pale-orange in colour, and always settles with closed wings, which have several black spots on the underside. It flies in a slow, lazy way for only a short distance before touching down again. Although in decline, it is still the commonest butterfly of upland acid grasslands from mid-June until early August.

Small tortoiseshell *(Aglais urticae)* **Trilliw bach**

This well-known hill-topping butterfly has orange and black patterned wings with a white spot at the tip of the forewing. It is one of the first butterflies to be seen in spring.

Painted lady. © Keith Noble.

Red admiral.

Ringlet. © Keith Noble.

Small heath. © Keith Noble.

Small tortoiseshell.

Caterpillars / Lindysyn

You are more likely to see the caterpillar than the moth!

Beautiful yellow underwing *(Anarta myrtilli)* *Ôl-adain felen hardd*
This striking caterpillar is bright green with white and yellow dashes along its body. It can be seen on heather moorland from May to September.

Emperor moth *(Saturnia pavonia)* *Ymerawdwr*
This slightly hairy caterpillar can be found on heather between June and August. Initially black, it becomes greener as it gets older, with black bands around each segment of its body. Dots on its back mimic heather buds and change colour as the heather grows, starting greenish-yellow and becoming purple.

Fox moth *(Macrothylacia rubi)* *Gwyfyn y cadno*
This large, hairy caterpillar can be seen from July to April on upland grassland and moorland. Fully grown caterpillars can be 7cm long, with long brown hairs on the sides of the body and shorter dark orange hairs along the back. The hair tips are toxic and can cause skin irritation, and although the severity of the reaction varies and some people seem to be immune. It is probably best not to handle them.

Beautiful yellow underwing caterpillar. © Sam Bosanquet.

Young emperor moth caterpillar.

Old emperor moth caterpillar. © Graham Motley.

Fox moth caterpillar.

Moths / Gwyfynod

Moths are notoriously difficult to see – partly because they mainly only fly at night. However, even day flying moths tend to be under-recorded simply because they rarely stay still! Here are five that you may see.

Antler *(Cerapteryx graminis)* **Gwyfyn corn carw**
Found in acid grasslands between July and September, this distinctive, medium-sized, brown moth has a cream antler-like mark on its forewing. Found in open grassland habitats, it frequently flies during the morning, and often feeds on thistles.

Beautiful yellow underwing *(Anarta myrtilli)* **Ôl-adain felen hardd**
This small (22mm) moth has red-brown, marbled forewings with a small, central white blotch, and black bordered, yellow hindwings. It can be seen on sunny days from April to August, flying rapidly and low over upland heather.

Common heath *(Ematurga atomaria)* **Gwyfyn y rhos**
As the name suggests, this small, pale coloured, day-flying moth is common on heather moorland from May to August. Although it often has dark brown bands on its forewings, these are sometimes merged or even absent. It usually rests with its wings held flat, and will fly up if disturbed.

Emperor *(Saturnia pavonia)* **Ymerawdwr**
This large, fluffy moth has a wingspan of up to 10cm and is often mistaken for a butterfly. It is unmistakeable as it is the only large moth with big spots on all four wings. Males are grey-brown, have feathery antennae, and spend most of their time flying fast over heather. Females are bluish-grey and spend most of their time sitting on heather waiting for the males! It can be seen during April and May.

Antler moth.

Beautiful yellow underwing moth. © Patrick Clement (CC BY 2.0).

Common heath moth. © Keith Noble.

Emperor moth. © Sam Bosanquet.

Fox moth. © Rasbak (CC BY 3.0).

Fox moth *(Macrothylacia rubi)* *Gwyfyn y cadno*

This large brown moth is found on heathland in May and June. Like the emperor moth, the males have feathery antennae, and fly rapidly just above the ground on sunny afternoons searching for the larger females, which are nocturnal.

Beetles / Chwilod

There are hundreds of different beetles in the National Park, many of which can be seen in upland habitats. Here are six that you may encounter.

Coppery click beetle *(Ctenicera cuprea)* *Chwilen glec*
There are more than 60 different species of click beetle, and at 1cm long, this is one of the largest. Found on rough grassland from May to August, its narrow, metallic coppery-purple body and long, toothed antennae make it easy to identify. Click beetles make a clicking noise when they jump and can leap out of danger even when they are on their backs!

Dor beetle *(Geotrupes stercorarius)* *Chwilod Dor*
This is the archetypal beetle, with a shiny, oval, domed body and a blue sheen; shiny black legs with noticeable spikes, and longitudinally grooved wing cases. Commonly known as dung beetles, they belong to a sub-family called scarabs, which were regarded as sacred by the ancient Egyptians.

Froghopper *(Philaenus spumarius)* *Llyffant y Gwair Cyffredin*
Although not strictly a beetle, the froghopper may be mistaken for one as it holds its wings together over its body. More correctly classed together with cicadas, these amazing small, brown insects can leap 70cm into the air when threatened – the equivalent of a human jumping over a tower block! Although the adults may not be familiar, their tiny, green nymphs or 'spittlebugs' certainly are, as during the spring and summer, they hide in a mass of foamy bubbles known variously as 'cuckoo spit', 'frog spit' or 'snake spit'.

Rose chafer *(Cetonia aurata)* *Chwilen rosod*
Rose chafers are large, broad beetles found along the upland edge. They have metallic coppery-green bodies with creamy-white streaks on the wing case, and they love to feed on dog roses. They are very noisy in flight, and are most commonly spotted during warm, sunny days in summer and autumn.

Click beetle. © Sam Bosanquet.

Cuckoo spit.

Dor beetle.

Rose chafer.

Violet ground beetle.

Violet ground beetle *(Carabus violaceus) chwilen fioled llawr*

The large violet ground beetle is a nocturnal predator, which hunts smaller invertebrates and 'pest' species such as slugs. It is black with a distinctive metallic purple sheen, especially around the flattened edges of its wing cases, and can grow to 3cm long. It rests during the day in leaf litter and under logs and stones, and can be found from March to October.

Spiders / Corynnod

There are over 600 species of spider in the UK, and more than half of them are tiny – less than 3mm long! Although they are common in the uplands, especially in spring, you are more likely to see the webs than the spiders. They are not insects but arachnids, and I've included a couple of the larger and more common ones here.

Cave spiders *(Meta menardi* and *Meta merianae) Copyn yr ogof*
You are only likely see these spiders if you venture into a cave. They are one of the largest spiders found in the UK. *Meta menardi* is dark brown and has a body up to 1.5cm long (not including the legs!), but as it likes to live in total darkness (or at least areas where there is no direct light), it often goes unnoticed. You are more likely to see the similar but smaller *Meta merianae*, which is brown and grey and often found in crevices a short distance inside cave entrances. Although the adult spiders are repelled by sunlight, young cave spiders are attracted to it, which enables them to leave the cave and find somewhere new to populate.

Garden spider *(Araneus diadematus) Copyn y groes*
This common spider can be found almost everywhere between June and November and is easily recognised by the large white cross on its abdomen. The females are up to 1.2cm long – twice the size of the males, which they sometimes mistake for prey! They build classic 'orb' spider webs, often in rush or sedge, then sit in the middle and wait for their prey to become trapped in the sticky threads. Once trapped, the prey is wrapped tightly in silk before being killed with a venomous bite.

Cave spider web.

Garden spider.

Wolf spider with egg-sac.

Wolf spider *(Pardosa amentata)* *Copyn y blaidd*

This medium-sized spider hunts on the ground during the day, chasing its prey and leaping on it, just like a wolf. It is quite hairy, comes in various patterns of brown, dark grey and black, and can sometimes be seen sunbathing or running across the ground. The female often carries a large round egg-sac underneath the back end of her body and will carry her young on her back for a few days after they hatch.

Frog.

Frog spawn.

AMPHIBIANS / AMFFIBIAIDD

For quick identification:

Frogs = smooth skinned; hop and jump rather than crawl and walk; spawn laid in clumps.
Toads = warty skinned; crawl and walk rather than hop and jump; spawn laid in long strings.

Frog *(Rana temporaria) broga*

Usually brown or grey with smooth skin and long back legs covered in dark bands, frogs spend much of the year on dry land, often in woodland, hedge-rows and tussocky grassland, where they feed on a variety of invertebrates and smaller amphibians. They return to their birthplace – often upland ponds – as early as February to mate and lay clumps of spawn, and some pools can contain so many frogs that the surface appears to seethe. Indeed, small pools can become so crowded that some frogs are forced to spawn in shallow puddles. Although the spawn may contain thousands of eggs, only a few tadpoles will survive, the vast majority being eaten by birds or fish, or dying due to desiccation (as a result of their habitat drying out).

Common toad.

Common toad *(Bufo bufo)* ***Llyffant dafadennog***

Although you will find toads in the same ponds as frogs, and at the same time of year, they prefer to breed in larger, deeper ponds. Olive-brown, with warty skin and short back legs, they walk rather than hop, and lay their spawn in long strings, often wrapped around the stems of aquatic plants. Dozens of toads may migrate back to their breeding ponds on the first warm, damp evening of the year, traditionally around St Valentine's Day. They are carnivores, feeding largely on insects which they catch on the wing using a long, sticky tongue.

Palmate newt.

Palmate newt *(Triturus helvetica)* *Madfall ddŵr balfog*

The palmate newt is the UK's smallest newt (less than 9cm long) and is more likely to be found in ponds in upland areas and moorlands than other newt species. It has a peach-coloured underside with a few spots on its belly but none on its throat. Between March and July, adult males develop black webs on their hind feet and a thin filament at the end of their tail. They breed in ponds during the spring, spend the summer feeding on invertebrates in woodland and tussocky grassland, and hibernate underground during the winter, often under tree roots or in dry-stone walls.

Adder.

REPTILES /
YMLUSGIAD

There are six species of reptile native to the UK, of which four occur in the National Park. Sadly, these fascinating animals are becoming increasingly rare, and all are now protected under Schedule 5 of the Wildlife and Countryside Act 1981.

Adder *(Vipera berus)* *Gwiber*

Britain's only venomous snake, adders may grow to almost a metre in length and can often be seen on warm days basking in the sun, especially in semi-open heathland and rocky upland areas. They live on small mammals – frogs, toads and lizards – and will even eat worms and insects if hungry. The males are light grey with a black zigzag along their back, and they are particularly active in April after they have come out of hibernation, when they can sometimes be seen wrestling with each other as they seek out mates. The females are browner. The bite, although painful, is rarely fatal for humans (although it can kill an over-inquisitive dog). However, you should seek medical attention if bitten.

Adders are fairly reclusive – it is probably fair to say that they are more frightened of you than you of them! To the Druids they represented renewal, a symbolism probably related to the fact they shed their skins.

Welsh folklore tells that parts of their body applied in various ways will alleviate a huge range of illnesses. Indeed, as late as the 19th century dried adder skin was thought to cure rheumatism, thorn pricks and headaches, and well into the 20th century powdered adder skin was considered beneficial to the spleen and a cure for constipation.

Common lizard *(Zootoca vivipara)* **Madfall**

The common lizard lives further north than any other species of non-marine reptile, and is found across many habitats including heathland, moorland, woodland and grassland. Although it is the UK's most common reptile, it is also very alert and shy and sightings are rare, although it can sometimes be spotted basking in the sun on a warm spring day. They hibernate underground or in log-piles between September and March, the males emerging a few weeks before the females. The species is unusual among reptiles as they give birth to live young rather than laying eggs, so it's also known as the viviparous lizard. When newborn, young lizards are about 4cm long, dark brown or black. Adult males have bright yellow or orange undersides covered in black spots, whereas females have grey, yellow or green undersides with no spots. They grow to about 15cm in length and can live for up to 12 years. Common lizards hunt insects, spiders, snails and earthworms, which they stun by shaking and then swallowing whole. If attacked, they can shed their tails, which eventually grow back as a short-pointed stub.

Grass snake *(Natrix natrix)* **Neidr fraith**

The grass snake is the UK's largest snake, growing to 1.5 metres in length. Greenish in colour, with a yellow collar and black neck patches, females are bigger than males. Grass snakes are strong swimmers and favour wetland habitats, or at least somewhere with a pond or stream nearby, and during the summer months they can often be seen swimming. They feed almost exclusively on amphibians but will sometimes take small fish or even the odd small mammal. Like all reptiles, grass snakes hibernate (usually from October to April).

Common lizard.

Slow worm. © Julie Bell.

Grass snake.

Slow worm *(Anguis fragilis)* **Neidr ddefaid**

Despite being commonly identified as a snake, the slow worm is in fact a legless lizard. The two biggest give-aways are that slow worms have eyelids (which snakes do not), and that they can shed their tails. They are also much smaller than snakes, with smooth, golden-grey skin. Males are paler and sometimes have blue spots; females are larger with dark sides and a dark stripe down the back. They are found in heathland, tussocky grassland, woodland edges, and limestone pavements, preferring locations where they can find a sunny patch in which to sunbathe and catch plenty of invertebrates to eat. If a predator attempts to eat them they stay completely still and shed their tail, which wriggles for up to 15 minutes. The predator generally picks up the tail and moves away, leaving the tailless slow worm alive. The tail soon regenerates into a short, pointed stub.

Great black slug.

SLUGS AND SNAILS / GWLITHOD A MALWOD

Snails and slugs are both gastropods. The most obvious difference between them is that snails have shells and slugs do not. There are about 30 species of slug in the UK, and over 100 species of snail, but many are only distinguishable by dissection.

In the mountains, the most common slug – the great black – belongs to a complex species that can only be 100% differentiated by dissecting its genitalia. The slugs in this species range in size from 7.5–18cm long, and in colour from black and grey through dark brown to orange or even red. Some of these slugs are omnivorous, eating carrion and dung as well as rotting vegetation. Although largely nocturnal, they can often be seen feeding on upland grassland and moorland after daytime rain.

Buzzard (and below). © Steve Wilce
breconbeaconsbirder.com

BIRDS / ADAR

The Brecon Beacons National Park is famous for its birdlife ... and with good reason. Over 200 different birds have been recorded here, about 100 of which breed in the Park, including some nationally endangered species. Although spring is generally a good time to see them – particularly the 30 or so species of woodland birds because the trees are not yet in full leaf – some summer visitors are yet to arrive. Indeed, while many are resident all year, others only come to breed in summer, and yet more use the Park as a migration stopover and will be around for only short periods.

For more information on birds, the RSPB website is excellent (www.rspb. org.uk); and if you think you see something unusual, please relay your sightings to the county recorder or the British Trust for Ornithology 'Bird Track' (www.bto.org).

While far from exhaustive, the following list includes many of the birds you are most likely to encounter.

Buzzard *(Buteo buteo) Bwncath*
One of two large birds of prey resident in the Park (the other being the red kite), the buzzard's mewling call is unmistakeable. Buzzards have broad, rounded wings with finger-like feathers at the ends, a short neck and a rounded tail (not forked), which is often fanned when it soars. The female is larger than the male. Despite their size, they are often mobbed by crows

that see them as a threat. Their main diet is small mammals, but if food is scarce they will also take reptiles, amphibians, birds, large insects and even earthworms. Their nest is a substantial structure of branches and twigs, up to a metre wide, usually built in trees but also on rocky crags. Wingspan = 110–130cm.

Carrion crow *(Corvus corone)* **Brân dyddyn**
Clever and adaptable, carrion crows are found almost everywhere. Unlike rooks (which are gregarious), crows are solitary and are usually seen alone or in pairs. They eat almost anything – carrion, scraps, eggs, worms, insects, seeds and fruit. Their most common call is a guttural "kraa-kraa-kraa". The Celts believed that crows followed the sun as it sank into hell each evening and regarded them as symbols of death or evil. Wingspan = 95–105cm.

Chiffchaff *(Phylloscopus collybitus)* **Siff-siaff**
The chiffchaff is an olive-brown bird about the size of a blue-tit, with a song like its name. It is one of the first songbirds to appear in spring, arriving in March and staying until September, although some over-winter in the lowlands. It appears nervous, flitting rapidly through the treetops and constantly flicking its tail. It eats insects and spiders which it picks from the branches, although it will sometimes take them in flight. Wingspan = 15–20cm.

Carrion crow. © Steve Wilce
breconbeaconsbirder.com

Chiffchaff. © Steve Wilce
breconbeaconsbirder.com

Cuckoo. © Steve Wilce
breconbeaconsbirder.com

Curlew. © Steve Wilce
breconbeaconsbirder.com

Cuckoo *(Cuculus canorus) Cog*

You are more likely to hear a cuckoo than to see one, especially along up-land edges with hawthorns and sparse tree cover. A brief summer visitor, cuckoos are here between mid-April and mid-June. They are pigeon-sized birds with a sleek, grey-blue body, dark striped white under parts, a long tail, and pointed wings. They eat insects and love hairy caterpillars. In the Brecon Beacons area, the female lays her eggs almost exclusively in the nests of meadow pipits. Wingspan = 55–65cm.

Curlew *(Numenius arquata) Gylfinir*

Curlews are large wading birds, found in open moorland and boggy ground from April to July. Numbers have declined significantly in recent years. They are easily recognised by their long, down-curved bills, mottled brown feathers and long legs, and by their unique, hauntingly wavering or bubbling display calls. They eat a range of insects including leatherjackets, beetles, caterpillars and worms. Wingspan = 80–100cm.

Dipper *(Cinclus cinclus)* **Bronwen y dŵr**

An unmistakeable medium-size bird of fast-flowing upland streams and rivers, the plump dipper is dark-brown with a white bib and a short tail. Usually seen bobbing up and down on a stone in the middle of a stream, or flying low and fast with whirring wings, it feeds on aquatic insect larvae and freshwater shrimps and happily walks into (and under) raging torrents to find them. It nests under rocky overhangs or even behind waterfalls. Wingspan = 25–30cm.

Dotterel *(Charadrius morinellus)* **Hutan mynydd**

This colourful medium-sized plover has traditional stopover sites in the Park, particularly where rocky terrain occurs on rounded hill-tops and whale-back ridges, such as in the Carmarthen Fan and the Black Mountains. They can be seen between early April and mid-May, and sometimes return to the same areas in early autumn. They are often very confident and allow you to get quite close to them. They have a wingspan of about 60cm, a grey-brown back and a bright chestnut belly with a white band above, a white throat, and a dark head cap with a white stripe below. They eat insects and worms. Although they are often solitary, groups (or 'trips') of up to 20 birds are not uncommon.

Fieldfare *(Turdus pilaris)* **Caseg y ddrycin**

A large, colourful thrush, the sociable fieldfare spends the winter in flocks of anything from twenty to several hundred, roaming the countryside in search of food. Although predominantly a lowland bird, they can often be seen in autumn on the upland edge in the company of **redwings**, stripping berries from hawthorn and rowan trees. They arrive from late October, and as winter progresses their diet switches to foraging on the ground for worms and invertebrates. They have mostly gone by April. Wingspan = about 40cm.

Dipper. © Steve Wilce
breconbeaconsbirder.com

Dotterel. © Steve Wilce
breconbeaconsbirder.com

Fieldfares. © Steve Wilce
breconbeaconsbirder.com

Golden plover. © Steve Wilce
breconbeaconsbirder.com

Golden plover *(Pluvialis apricaria) Chwilgorn y mynydd*

Golden plovers have distinctive gold and black summer plumage, and often run in short, nervous bursts with a stiff, erect stance. Although only small numbers breed in the uplands here, you will know if they have breeding intentions by hearing a single repeated 'peeeep' call. If you hear this between May and July, move away as the birds may be breeding nearby. In winter, they lose their black feathers and move to the upland edges, frequenting rolling countryside such as Mynydd Illtyd where they gather in large flocks containing upwards of 300 birds. During the day they roost tightly together on short open grassland or cut bracken, and at dusk they fly as a tight flock to neighbouring farmland to feed on worms, beetles and insects. Wingspan = 65–75cm.

Young great spotted woodpecker.
© Steve Wilce breconbeaconsbirder.com

Green woodpecker. © Steve Wilce
breconbeaconsbirder.com

Great spotted woodpecker *(Dendrocopos major) Cnocell fraith fwyaf*

A black-and-white bird with a red patch under its tail, this woodpecker has a distinctive bouncing flight and rarely ventures far from old broadleaved woodland where it spends a lot of time clinging to branches and hiding on the opposite side of the tree to the observer! You are most likely to be alerted to its presence by hearing it 'drumming' away at a tree trunk, either excavating its nest or looking for insects and larvae which it catches with its sticky tongue. Wingspan = 35–40cm.

Green woodpecker *(Picus viridis) Cnocell y coed*

Green woodpeckers are unmistakeable. Pigeon-sized, they are olive-green with a red crown and black eyes. They nest in holes that they excavate in broadleaved trees and come out of the woods to feed on the ground, mostly on ants, which they devour by the thousand. They have a loud, laughing 'yaffle' call. Wingspan = just over 40cm.

Grey wagtail. © Steve Wilce
breconbeaconsbirder.com

Kestrels.

Grey wagtail *(Motacilla cinerea)* *Siglen las*

The unexpectedly colourful grey wagtail has a very long, black and white tail and a bright yellow underside. During summer months, they are common near fast-flowing upland rivers where they nest in hollows and crevices lined with moss and twigs. They eat insects such as ants and midges and will sometimes take tadpoles from the water. Wingspan = about 25cm.

Kestrel *(Falco tinnunculus)* *Cudyll coch*

This bird of prey can be seen perched on a pole or a tree on the boundary between open ground and woodland. Reddish-brown on top and paler underneath, it has a long grey tail and pointed wings, and is the only bird of prey that can hover in a stationary position. It eats mainly voles and needs to catch 4–8 of these every day, often catching several in succession and then saving some to eat just before it roosts. A permanent resident, kestrels do not build their own nests, but use old or disused stick nests, ledges on cliffs, or holes in trees. Wingspan = 70–80cm.

Lapwing *(Vanellus vanellus) Cornicyll*

Also known as peewits because of their call, lapwings are easily recognised when on the ground by their crest and black and white plumage. The male has a spectacular song-flight: wobbling, zigzagging, rolling and diving while calling to advertise his presence. They like to breed in damp, upland areas where they have a constant supply of insects, and it is not uncommon to see them in rhôs pasture. In autumn, they descend to the lowland where they mix with flocks of over-wintering European birds to feed in pasture and on arable fields, looking for worms. Wingspan = 85cm.

Meadow pipit *(Anthus pratensis) Pibydd y waun*

This small, streaky yellow-brown bird is the most common songbird in the uplands, although nationally its numbers are in serious decline. Easily confused with the slightly larger **skylark**, it can be distinguished by its fluttering flight (skylarks are more stiff-winged) and by its white outer tail-feathers, often seen as it flies away. They like open country, and in spring and summer they breed in upland areas, constructing a well-concealed nest from dry grass, often lined with hair. In autumn they move south to more lowland areas, and some migrate to continental Europe. They eat flies, moths, beetles and spiders. Wingspan = 22–25cm.

Merlin *(Falco columbarius) Cudyll bach*

The Merlin is the UK's smallest bird of prey. It has a long, square-cut tail and broad-based pointed wings, and it flies rapidly, beating its wings furiously and occasionally gliding with wings held close to the body. It breeds in the uplands between April and September, and unlike its continental cousins, most Welsh merlins nest on the ground. Although they will take small mammals and insects, they eat mainly small birds, which they hunt by perching on rocks or trees, or even on the backs of grazing sheep! The prey is usually caught by surprise after a short distance, low-level flight from the perch. However, if this doesn't work, they may resort to vertical stooping or persistent chasing. In late autumn, they leave their upland breeding sites and descend to the lowlands where they are joined by Icelandic birds which over-winter here. Wingspan = 50–60cm.

Lapwing. © Steve Wilce
breconbeaconsbirder.com

Meadow pipit. © Steve Wilce
breconbeaconsbirder.com

Merlin. © Steve Wilce
breconbeaconsbirder.com

Peregrine falcon. © Steve Wilce
breconbeaconsbirder.com

Peregrine falcon *(Falco peregrinus)* *Hebog glas*

These large, powerful falcons are fearsome killing machines, able to stoop on prey at over 300kph. They are slate-grey above and lighter below, with a white throat and cheeks, and a black moustache and mask. Their wings are long, broad and pointed, and their tail is relatively short. Weighing a hefty 1.25kg, they are able to take medium-sized birds such as small ducks, and they sometimes take mammals. However, their favourite food is wood-pigeon which they often take on the wing, the contact being accompanied by a loud 'bang' and an explosion of feathers. Peregrines need open terrain for hunting but are restricted to areas where there are cliff-ledges, quarry faces or crags suitable for their nests, although they are adaptable and are increasingly found breeding in urban situations. The majority stay within 100km of their birthplace. Wingspan = 95–115cm.

Pied flycatcher. © Steve Wilce
breconbeaconsbirder.com

Raven. © Steve Wilce
breconbeaconsbirder.com

Pied flycatcher *(Ficedula hypoleuca) Gwybedog brith*

This summer visitor is black and white and slightly smaller than a sparrow. It can be seen in mature deciduous woodland, particularly oak woodland, between April and August, and the hillsides of Wales are something of a stronghold. It eats insects and caterpillars during the breeding season, and fruit and seeds at other times. Wingspan = 21–24cm.

Raven *(Corvus corax) Cigfran*

Ravens are big – bigger than buzzards – and can weigh as much as 1.5kg. From May onwards, small family parties are commonly seen soaring and playing along the highest ridges of the Central Beacons and Black Mountains. Although sometimes confused with the smaller carrion crow, they can be distinguished by their longer neck and diamond-shaped tail, and their distinctive 'cronk-cronk' call. They build their nests on cliffs and quarried faces, occasionally in large trees, and although they are great scavengers and eat mainly carrion, they will also take mammals, birds, eggs, insects, and invertebrates. Ravens are incredibly intelligent, and in autumn and winter they can be a real spectacle as they soar the ridges and turn on their backs to impress their partner. Larger groups of younger, non-breeding birds can often be found displaying around smaller hills such as Allt-yr-Esgair, Mynydd Troed, and Tor y Foel. Most birds are resident and rarely wander from their breeding areas. Wingspan = 120–150cm.

Red grouse scat.

Red grouse. © Colin Richards.

Red grouse *(Lagopus lagopus)* **Grugiar goch**

Red grouse are found in low numbers across upland heath throughout the area, and over the past few years there has been a gradual increase in their population here, even in areas where there is no positive management by upland land-owners. A plump, medium-sized game bird, they have reddish-brown plumage with paler feathers over their legs and feet, a short tail and a slightly hooked beak. They eat heather shoots, seeds, berries and insects, and nest on the ground in a shallow scrape concealed by vegetation. Although resident, they are more noticeable in the winter months as that is the season for display and calling. At other times they tend to hide in the vegetation until disturbed by walkers, flying off suddenly with a loud 'go-back go-back go-back' alarm call and whirring wingbeats, often followed by a low, gliding descent. You are probably more likely to see their droppings (*scat*) than the birds. Wingspan = 55–60cm.

Red kite *(Milvus milvus) Barcud*

It was not long ago that these magnificent birds were on the verge of national extinction due to persecution by gamekeepers and farmers, and for many years they were only found in central Wales. Nowadays, thanks to one of the world's longest-running protection and reintroduction programmes, they are becoming increasingly common throughout the UK, and can be seen in both upland and lowland habitats. With a reddish-brown body, angled wings and deeply forked tail, these graceful birds are unmistakable. They are very large, weighing up to 1.3kg, and although they eat mainly carrion, they are opportunistic and will occasionally take small mammals. They also fly for miles to visit feeding stations such as the Red Kite centre at Llanddeusant, which is one of the best places to see them at close quarters. Their nests are sited 15–20m above the ground in large trees. Constructed from dead twigs, they are lined with grass and sheep's wool, and during the breeding season they are decorated with all sorts of rubbish found nearby … crisp packets, carrier bags, baler twine, underwear and even toys! If breeding is successful, the nest is reused the following year, and nests that have been in use for several seasons can grow to a substantial size. Despite their apparent success, it is estimated that at least half our native Welsh kites die through the deliberate abuse of agricultural chemicals in illegal poisoned bait set for foxes or crows. Wingspan = 175–195cm.

Redstart *(Phoenicurus phoenicurus) Tingoch*

A robin-sized bird, redstarts are identifiable by their quivering, bright orange-red tails and their bobbing movement. They can be seen from April to September feeding on insects, spiders, worms and berries in oak wood-land. They rarely spend much time on the ground. Wingspan = 20–25cm.

Redwing *(Turdus iliacus) Coch dan-aden*

The redwing is the UK's smallest thrush, with orange-red flank patches and a creamy stripe above the eye. It can be seen on the upland edges between November and March, when it gathers in large flocks, often with **fieldfares**, to strip hawthorn and rowan trees of their berries. Wingspan = 33–35cm.

Red kite. © Steve Wilce
breconbeaconsbirder.com

Redstart. © Steve Wilce
breconbeaconsbirder.com

Redwing. © Steve Wilce
breconbeaconsbirder.com

Ring ouzel. © Steve Wilce
breconbeaconsbirder.com

Ring ouzel *(Turdus torquatus)* *Mwyalchen y mynydd*

These rare birds are a delightful sight at places like the Craig Cerrig-gleisiad a Fan Frynych NNR and the Craig y Cilau NNR, where they inhabit the crags and gullies between March and October. Slightly smaller than a blackbird, the males are very distinctive, with black plumage, a pale wing panel and a striking white band across the top of their breast. Their nests are built on or very close to the ground, usually in heather, sometimes in a crevice and rarely in a tree, and when pairs have settled into their territories, a harsh 'chack' alarm call can give away their presence. The adults eat berries and insects, and their young are fed largely beetles and worms. Wingspan = about 40cm.

Skylark. © Steve Wilce
breconbeaconsbirder.com

Snipe. © Steve Wilce breconbeaconsbirder.com

Skylark *(Alauda arvensis) Ehedydd*

These streaky-brown songbirds are easily mistaken for **meadow pipits** until they start singing, and then they are unmistakeable! During a spectacular territorial song-flight, the bird rises almost vertically in the air, hovers for several minutes and then plummets. Song flights of up to an hour have been recorded, and the birds can climb 300 metres before descending. When they are not displaying, they can still be differentiated from pipits by their stiff-winged flight (pipits tend to flutter), and by their small crest, which is raised (and therefore more prominent) when the bird is alarmed. They eat seeds and insects, and are common in upland moorland from April to August, where they nest in a hollow on the ground, lined with grasses, leaves and hair. In winter they descend to open lowland farmland. Wingspan = 30–35cm.

Snipe *(Gallinago gallinago) Gïach*

Snipe are small, mottled brown wading birds with pale stripes on their back, dark stripes on their chest, and a pale belly. They have short legs and a disproportionately long straight bill, which they use to probe for worms and insect larvae. They were once common on wet upland moorlands between April and August, but sadly they are becoming more rare. If you are lucky, early in the season you may hear the males making an unusual 'drumming' sound, caused by their tail feathers vibrating during acrobatic flight displays. In winter they skulk around the edges of pools in vegetated wetlands where they are often joined by over-wintering birds from northern Europe. In a good year these can flush from wetter areas in large numbers when disturbed by walkers; more commonly you will see single birds that rapidly fly away with a jinking flight. Wingspan = 40–45cm.

Sparrowhawk. © Steve Wilce
breconbeaconsbirder.com

Stonechat. © Steve Wilce
breconbeaconsbirder.com

Sparrowhawk *(Accipiter nisus)* *Gwalch glas*

These pigeon-sized birds of prey are well adapted for hunting in confined spaces like dense woodland where they catch mainly birds, although they also take bats. They have a narrow tail and rounded wings, and males and females are markedly different, with males having reddish-orange chest bars and a blue-grey back and wings, and the much larger females having grey-brown chest bars and a brown back and wings. The males try to impress the females by performing 'roller-coaster' flight displays in spring. Wingspan = 55–70cm.

Stonechat *(Saxicola torquatus)* *Clochdar y cerrig*

The robin-sized stonechats often flick their wings while perched on top of low bushes or bracken. They have a loud 'tac' call that sounds like two stones being tapped together, and they are often heard before being seen. Male birds have black heads with white around the side of their neck, a mottled brown back and orangey-red breasts. Female birds are duller, with no black on their heads and only an orange tinge to their chests. Although they can be found throughout the year, they tend to leave the uplands in winter, and can often be seen congregating along fences in late autumn while they wait for the right conditions to migrate to warmer areas. They are sometimes confused with slightly rarer **Whinchat** (*Saxicola rubetra*) *Crec yr eithin*, but these can be distinguished as they have a prominent white stripe above the eye. Wingspan: = 18–20cm.

Wheatear *(Oenanthe oenanthe)* **Tinwen y garreg**

One of the earliest migrants to arrive from Africa, sometimes appearing as early as February, wheatears are common in the uplands between March and October. A small, ground-dwelling bird, it tends to spend most of its time hopping or running around looking for insects and larvae, but when it flies it is recognisable by its white rump and the black 'T' on its tail. The male has a blue-grey back, a white belly, an orange breast, and black wings and cheeks. The female has a browner back. The nest-site is normally in a tumble of rocks or hidden beside boulders, and if you stray too close, both sexes will warn you off with a sharp 'tac' call. Once known as 'white arse', it is said that the modern name was coined by John Brown who, when asked by Queen Victoria to identify the bird, was too embarrassed to use the word 'arse'. Wingspan = 25–30cm.

Wood warbler *(Phylloscopus sibilatrix)* **Telor y coed**

This attractive warbler has bright green upper parts, a yellow throat and upper chest, and white under parts. It eats insects and is commonest in scrubby woodland and in the more western oak woods between April and August. Although it can be heard singing from the tops of trees, it nests in low scrub or even on the ground. Wingspan = 20–25cm.

Wren *(Troglodytes troglodytes)* **Dryw**

This tiny, dumpy brown bird packs a real punch when it sings! The most common UK breeding bird, it has a remarkably loud voice, and can be found almost anywhere as long as there are plenty of insects to eat. Its domed nest is built using moss and leaves in sheltered bushes and crevices among the rocks. It is so small that it is often overlooked until it scurries mouse-like along the ground. Wingspan = about 15cm.

Wheatear – male © Steve Wilce
breconbeaconsbirder.com

Wheatear – female © Steve Wilce
breconbeaconsbirder.com

Wood warbler. © Steve Wilce
breconbeaconsbirder.com

Wren. © Steve Wilce
breconbeaconsbirder.com

Wood mouse.

MAMMALS

Some of the more important mammals in the Park are the bats. Indeed, the largest roost of lesser horseshoe bats in Britain is in a cave on the Llangattock Escarpment overlooking Crickhowell. You can read more about bats in the section on Nocturnal Wanderings.

Small mammals

There are many small mammals living in this area. Although they are far more numerous on lowland farmland than on the surrounding hills, some venture towards the uplands where they can be found in the more sheltered valleys, in the ancient woodlands, and in the shelter of the dense vegetation of the heather moorlands.

The smallest species include the mice, shrews and voles. Although these can be easily mistaken for each other, there are some key characteristics that will help you distinguish them at a glance:

Mouse = Large eyes and ears, long tail, short pointed snout.

Shrew = Small eyes and ears, short tail, long pointed snout.

Vole = Small eyes and ears, short tail, rounded snout.

Wood mouse *(Apodemus sylvaticus) Llygoden y coed*

Our most common and widespread native rodent, wood mice, are found in most habitats, although they don't like the damp. They prefer woodlands and fields, and while they are rare in upland areas, they can sometimes be seen along the upland edge, especially where there is plenty of cover. Although nocturnal some individuals venture out in daylight, particularly in shady woodlands. They are small (no more than 10cm long) and their tails are as long as their bodies – which explains why they are also known as long-tailed field mice.

Most wood mice live in complicated burrows that include food stores and nest chambers made of leaves, moss and grass. Some burrows survive for several generations and are modified as required. In winter, the burrow entrance is often blocked with leaves, twigs or stones. Their diet includes seeds, green plants and fruits but they are very adaptable. For example, in a mixed deciduous wood they will eat acorns and seeds during the winter, buds in spring, caterpillars, worms and insects in summer, and blackberries and fungi in autumn. Spare food is cached in underground burrows, and many trees and shrubs germinate from forgotten wood mouse food stores.

Common shrew.

Bank vole.

Common shrew *(Sorex araneus)* *Llyg Cyffredin*

Common shrews are tiny: 5.5–8.5cm long, with a tail about half the length of their body. They have dense, velvety fur – dark brown on the back, pale brown on the sides, and silver-grey underneath – tiny eyes, tiny ears, a long pointy nose, and red teeth. They can be found in most habitats but prefer woodland and grassland. Shrews are carnivorous, eating insects, spiders, worms, slugs, amphibians and even small rodents. They need to consume about 250% of their body weight in food each day in order to survive and will starve if they go without food for more than a few hours. They are therefore active day and night, only taking short periods of rest between relatively long bursts of activity. They do not hibernate because their bodies are too small to store sufficient fat reserves, but they have evolved to survive on meagre rations through the winter as, incredibly, their skulls shrink by up to 20%, their brains get smaller by as much as 30%, and their spines get shorter. Their other organs also lose mass. They make their nests underground or under dense vegetation, and although adults may only live for a year, this is just long enough for them to have three of four litters of around six young. They are very territorial and aggressive for their size, and they can sometimes be heard making high-pitched squeaks as they fight.

Vole / *Llygoden*

Apart from the water vole (which is very rare and only found in lowland areas) there are two species of vole that you may see: **field vole** *(Microtus agrestis) Llygoden bengron y gwair* and **bank vole** *(Clethrionomys glareolus / Llygoden bengron goch)*. Field voles like grass, heath and moorland habitats, while bank voles prefer woodland and hedgerows. Field voles spend much of their time in their runs and burrows and eat seeds, roots and leaves, while bank voles are very active and eat fruit, nuts (especially hazelnuts) and small insects. Although voles rarely live for more than about a year, they can have three to six litters a year (of up to seven young each litter). Field voles are roughly 13cm long with a tail about one-third the length of their body, and are a greyish- or yellowish-brown, with a pale-grey underside. Bank voles are slightly smaller with a tail about half the length of their body, and are a richer, chestnut brown.

Mole hills.

Mole *(Talpa europaea)* *Twrch daear*

You are far more likely to see a molehill than a mole! These subterranean mammals are about 15cm long, with cylindrical bodies, a pointed pink snout, tiny eyes and ears, and velvety dark fur. Their powerful front paws have strong claws designed for digging, and moles have been known to dig their way through almost 15 metres of soil in an hour. Although they eat beetles and other insects, and will even take baby mice, their main food is earthworms, which they eat by the thousand. A mole needs to eat the equivalent of its own bodyweight each day. Their run acts like a trap, and when a worm falls into it, the mole bites its head. Their saliva contains a toxin which paralyses the worm, which is then stored in specially dug chambers for later consumption. Before eating it, the mole pulls the worm between its paws to force the earth out of its gut. Large molehills show the position of a nest, while a line of small molehills shows the location of a deep tunnel.

Otter. © Steve Wilce
breconbeaconsbirder.com

Otter *(Lutra lutra)* **Dwrgi**

Otters suffered a severe decline across the UK until they were made a protected species in 1981, since when they have been recovering. They can now be found in and around most of the waterways in the Park including some of the upland streams, and can even be seen in Brecon, Crickhowell and Llangynidr, where the River Usk flows through the towns. However, this charismatic mammal is very shy, and rarely emerges from cover except at dawn and dusk. Although you are just as likely to see a mink as an otter (see below), otters are much larger with more powerful bodies, a broad snout, and pale grey-brown fur. They have webbed feet and dense fur, and they can close their nose and ears when underwater. They live in sheltered bank-side holes (or 'holts'), usually in hollow spaces among bank-side tree roots, but they will happily use other structures that offer seclusion and a quick exit into the river, including artificially made sites. They also construct temporary shelters called 'hovers'. They are one of Wales' top predators, feeding mainly on fish and eels, but also taking waterfowl, amphibians and crustaceans. You can tell when they are around as they leave chunky paw prints called 'pug marks', somewhat like a dog's, but with five toes. They also leave piles of fish remains, and faeces (called spraints), which have a musky smell like fresh hay.

Mink *(Neovison vison)* *Minc*

The American mink is not native and is a real pest! A medium-sized member of the weasel family, this small, agile and adaptable marauder has no predators, and since its release into the UK (both deliberately and accidentally), has readily adapted to living here. It can swim, run and climb and will eat almost anything, including fish, amphibians, reptiles, waterfowl and small mammals. Never having had to contend with such a successful predator, our native wildlife has been unable to protect itself. It is the mink that is largely responsible for the catastrophic decline in the number of water voles. Mink can be distinguished from otters by their smaller size, darker fur, and white chin and throat. They live in dens, often close to water in the eroded roots of oaks, sycamores or willows, and live for up to three years in the wild. They are fairly common in the Waterfall Country in the south of the Park.

Brown hare *(Lepus europaeus)* *Ysgyfarnog*

Brown hares were once a common sight on the open grasslands and heaths – a habitat they favour as it allows them to spot potential predators. They are now far less common, their numbers having been affected not only by habitat loss, but also by hare coursing. They are a golden-brown colour, with a pale belly, very long black-tipped ears, large powerful hind legs, and a black-topped, white-bottomed tail. They do not burrow, but shelter in shallow depressions in the ground called 'forms'. If disturbed, they bound away in a zigzag pattern. They are most commonly seen in grassland at woodland edges and are at their most visible in early spring as the breeding season encourages fighting or 'boxing' – hence the phrase 'as mad as a march hare'. Brown hares are herbivores and feed on young broadleaved plants, grasses and cereal crops, berries, fungi and roots. They will often eat herbs in the summer, and then switch to grasses in the winter. Although generally solitary, hares sometimes form loose groups when feeding.

Mink.

Brown hare. © Steve Wilce breconbeaconsbirder.com

Large mammals

Welsh Mountain sheep *(Ovis aries) Dafad Mynydd Cymreig*

Sheep outnumber humans about 3:1 in the National Park, and you can't venture far without seeing them. They are mainly Welsh Mountain sheep, a breed that has been around since the Middle Ages, although one variety, the Badger Face, has origins dating back to the 1st century, making it one of the oldest breeds in the world. They are small, hardy, and incredibly sure-footed, and can easily pick their way across rock and scree, find shelter in stormy weather, dig through snow, climb walls, push through small gaps, cross bogs and find sufficient food in the paltriest pastures. They are also surprisingly intelligent – there are stories of Welsh Mountain sheep rolling across cattle grids to reach better pasture!

True Welsh Mountain sheep are white with a white face and legs, with no wool on their forehead and cheeks, or below the knee joint. Their fleece is thick and quite long, and their tails are not normally docked. You may also see one of several varieties – the Badger Face Welsh Mountain (either white with a dark face and belly, or black with a white belly and white stripes over the eyes), the Balwen Welsh Mountain (black or brown with a white blaze on the face, white socks and a part-white tail), and Black Welsh Mountain sheep, which are entirely black. The South Wales Mountain is slightly larger, with tan markings on its legs and face, and a brown collar. The fleece of the Welsh Mountain sheep differs considerably in quality across the range of varieties – some is good, some is poor. However, the meat is consistently excellent and much sought after.

Welsh Mountain sheep.

Balwen Welsh Mountain sheep.

Welsh Mountain ponies. © Andrew Walters.

Welsh Mountain pony *(Equus caballus)* *Merlod Mynydd Cymreig*
One of the world's oldest and prettiest horse breeds and an iconic sight across the entire Park, Welsh Mountain ponies have been running free in the local uplands since Roman times. For generations, the harsh climate and poor grazing meant only the strongest, fittest and most intelligent individuals survived. However, Welsh Mountain ponies are now classified as a rare breed as there are only about 800 registered breeding mares left. Short and sturdy, these ponies are well-adapted to living in the Welsh mountains. They have an even but spirited temperament, and are dependable, friendly and incredibly hardy. They are renowned for their stamina, endurance and intelligence, and although they are no longer used as draft or pit ponies, they are still widely used at Welsh riding centres, where their gentle nature makes them perfect. Nowadays, however, their main job here is more prosaic. They are out on the open hill, wandering in herds and grazing the uplands. Tougher and less fussy eaters than sheep, Welsh Mountain ponies are ideal for keeping the uplands in good condition and, because they are hardy enough to spend winter on the hill, they graze all year round.

Red deer.

Red deer *(Cervus elaphus)* *Carw coch*

Although no one knows exactly how many wild deer there are in the National Park, there is at least one herd of red deer roaming free in Fforest Fawr, and they can sometimes be seen on the slopes of Fan Gyhirych and Fan Nedd. Locals would have us believe that this herd formed when deer, released from a local venison farm that went out of business, met up with a stag that had escaped from Margam Park near Swansea. Be that as it may, the deer population is increasing. The largest land mammal in Britain, they graze on grasses, heather and wimberries, as well as lichens and mosses. In summer they feed mainly at dawn and dusk, and rest during the day. During winter they spend most of the day searching for food and will eat tree shoots and bark and forage in farmland – something that brings them into conflict with farmers and foresters. The Celts believed that stags were symbols of renewal and rebirth because they shed their antlers every spring and these immediately started to grow again. White stags (or harts) were thought to have magical qualities, a notion reflected in the large number of pubs still called The White Hart.

Fox. © Colin Richards.

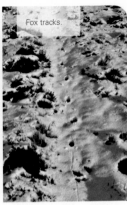
Fox tracks.

Red fox *(Vulpes vulpes)* *Llwynog coch*

Foxes are common across the region, but although they can be found in almost every habitat, you will only occasionally see one. It is far more common to hear them; dog foxes have a characteristic double bark while, particularly in the winter-mating season, females utter an eerie, spine-chilling scream. Growing to a length of about 70cm, foxes have orangey-red backs and heads, black tipped ears, white bellies, dark brown feet and a bushy, white-tipped orange tail (or 'brush') that can add another 40cm to their length. They are the only type of dog capable of retracting their claws like a cat. One of the reasons that they are so successful is that they are willing to eat almost anything – small mammals, birds and birds' eggs, insects, frogs, earthworms, grasshoppers, beetles, berries, fruit, and carrion. Anything they cannot eat, they bury. Environmental conditions determine how long a wild fox lives, and although they can live for around 7–10 years, in upland areas their life expectancy is short – rarely more than 3 years. It is estimated that in areas where lethal fox control is applied by farmers, up to 80% of the fox population is less than a year old. If you are lucky enough, you may see cubs romping and wrestling near their home on the upland edge at dawn or dusk during the summer months, which is a delightful experience. The Celts worshipped the fox for its fiery coat and cunning nature. In folklore, Welsh people believe it is lucky to see a single fox but unlucky to see several at once. Fox fat was once used to cure gout, rheumatism and baldness.

Nightjar. © Steve Wilce breconbeaconsbirder.com

Common pipistrelle. © Hugh Clark www.bats.org.uk

NOCTURNAL WANDERINGS

The Brecon Beacons National Park is a Dark Sky Reserve, and on a clear, moonless night, the stars are amazing. When the moon is full, it is sometimes possible to walk by moonlight – the ethereal silver light giving you a new perspective, despite being of familiar places. Even if you have no desire to walk through the night, walking at dawn or dusk has much to recommend it, for as the light decreases, so your other senses become more acute, and the scents and sounds of the landscape become more intense. You are also likely to come across wildlife that is not so apparent during the day.

Glow-worm *(Lampyris noctiluca)* *Tân bach diniwed*

Although male glow-worms look like typical beetles, the females have no wings and resemble their larvae. Rarely seen during the day, they climb up plant stems at night and emit an unmistakeable greenish-orange light in order to attract mates. The larvae and eggs can also emit light. These are best seen on dark nights in June and July in limestone country, such as the Craig y Cilau National Nature Reserve (NNR) near Crickhowell.

Nightjar (*Caprimulgus europaeus*) *Troellwr mawr*

You are more likely to hear a nightjar than see it – the males make a weird 'churring' clicking sound that rises and falls in an unmistakeable way. These nocturnal birds arrive in late April and are best seen (and heard) at dusk on warm, still summer evenings. They look a little like kestrels, with a long tail and pointed wings (wingspan about 60cm), and grey-brown mottled plumage which makes them almost impossible to see during the day. Usually found on heaths and moors, they also use recently cleared conifer plantations. They eat mainly moths and beetles.

Bats / Ystlumod

The only true flying mammals, bats make up almost a quarter of the 4,500 mammal species found worldwide. Nine species of bats have been recorded in the Park: below are the three that you are most likely to encounter.

Common pipistrelle (*Pipistrellus pipistrellus*) *Ystlum lleiaf*

There are three species of pipistrelle in the UK, the common pipistrelle being the smallest and most common. They mostly feed on midges, moths and other flying insects which they find in the dark by using echo-location, and a single pipistrelle can consume up to 3,500 midges in one night! In summer they roost in trees, and in winter they hibernate in buildings. Although you are unlikely to see one close-up, they have a characteristic rapid flight with lots of twists and turns.

Lesser horseshoe bat.
© Vincent Wildlife Trust

Noctule. © Hugh Clark www.bats.org.uk

Lesser horseshoe *(Rhinolophus hipposideros)* *Ystlum pedol lleiaf*

Only slightly larger than the pipistrelle, the lesser horseshoe bat is about the size of a plum with a characteristic horseshoe-shaped, fleshy nose. Although they are predominantly cave-dwellers, in summer they also roost in stables and barns and in the attics of large, old houses. They can sometimes be seen at dusk emerging from cave entrances in sheltered, wooded valleys, or flying along hedgerows and rivers, which they use as corridors between roosts and foraging areas. In winter, they hibernate in caves, and one of the largest roosts of lesser horseshoe bats in Britain is in Ogof Agen Allwedd, a huge cave system under Mynydd Llangatwg to the south of Crickhowell.

Noctule *(Nyctalus noctula)* *Ystlum Mawr*

In contrast to the previous bats, the noctule is one of the largest British bats, with an average wingspan of just under 40cm. A fast and powerful flier, it dives and zooms to feed on mayflies, moths and flying beetles, and they are often seen out in the open at dusk on summer evenings. They roost in holes in trees, and like the other bats they hibernate between about November and April.

Owls / Tylluanod

Powerful predators, owls have a totally silent flight, so you are unlikely to see one unless you are looking in the right direction at the right time. Although not upland birds, you will almost certainly hear them along the upland edge. There are many superstitions about owls – they are credited (incorrectly) with great intelligence, and the hooting of an owl was often considered to be an omen of death.

Barn owl *(Tyto alba)* *Tylluan wen*

Barn owls do not hoot, but produce an eerie, ear-shattering 'shree' scream. With a wingspan of about 90cm, they are slightly smaller than tawny owls and their plumage is much paler. You may see one at dawn or dusk, flying silently like a ghost while hunting mainly mice, voles, shrews.

Short-eared owl *(Asio flammeus)* *Tylluan glustiog*

Sometimes seen flying over open grassland and marsh during the day in autumn, the short-eared owl is sandy-brown with pale underwings and rounded wing-tips. It has a buoyant flight, generally flying low and fast when hunting for voles ... its favourite food. It has a wingspan of about a metre.

Tawny owl *(Strix aluco)* *Tylluan frech*

These reddish-brown birds are fully nocturnal and are rarely seen during the day. They make the characteristic hooting sounds – 'kewick' and 'hoo-hoo' – and will occasionally hoot in the middle of the day. They hunt small mammals and birds and will sometimes take amphibians and fish. Like the short-eared owl, they have a wingspan of about a metre.

Barn owl. © Steve Wilce
breconbeaconsbirder.com

Short-eared owl. © Steve Wilce
breconbeaconsbirder.com

Tawny owl. © Steve Wilce
breconbeaconsbirder.com

HUMANS

Despite its wild feel and the vast tracts of apparently unspoilt upland, the landscape of the Brecon Beacons National Park is man-made – shaped by human activity over millennia. Both agriculture and industry have left an indelible mark.

Old farmstead.

Old sheep fold.

FARMING

Agriculture makes up by far the largest share of land use within the National Park, and farming plays an essential role in the development and maintenance of the current landscape. Farming has been going on here for millennia and has had a huge effect on the landscape we see today. The earliest farms were all in upland areas because the lowlands were originally either too wooded or too wet to make farming viable, and the remains of old upland farming settlements and ancient field boundaries can still be seen across the region. In more recent times, from about the Norman period onwards, large areas of woodland were cleared from the valleys in order to create pasture; thus the most intensive farming now occurs in the lowlands.

Common land

About one third of the National Park is common land, mostly unfenced land on hillsides and mountains. The term 'common' is sometimes misunderstood – commons are actually privately owned, and the term 'common' simply refers to the fact that certain people (commoners) have rights over it. The system dates back to Norman times, when commons were areas of land which were of little value to the barons who owned them. Rather than let the land go to waste, the barons offered villagers the right to use the land, usually on payment of a small rent. This system continues in the Brecon Beacons to this day, and the commons are still privately owned, although some are under the control of organisations such as the National Trust, the National Park Authority, and large private estates. Local farmers move their livestock onto the hills in summer, enabling them to use the more fertile valley fields to grow hay and silage crops, thus providing fodder for the winter; local Commoners' Associations decide when the livestock should be gathered from the hill into more sheltered areas for the winter.

This is not an easy way of life – many hill farmers work 12-hour days seven days a week for much of the year, yet the annual income of an average hill farm is often less than £20k, and that's the income of the farm, not the farmer! Additionally, the average age of hill farmers is creeping above 60 as their children often leave farming to seek more lucrative employment opportunities elsewhere. Of all the people employed in farming in the area, just 3% are under 35.

Upland commons are an essential part of the landscape, and many are Sites of Special Scientific Interest (SSSIs). However, grazing by different animals (sheep, cattle and ponies) and at different intensities affects the variety of plants and thus the biodiversity. For example, in areas where grazing levels have been historically high and dominated by sheep, many heathland species have been grazed to extinction. Without sheep there would certainly be more deciduous woodland areas along the upland edge, and as hill farming becomes more tenuous and the number of grazing animals decreases, so the hillsides are starting to become pockmarked with thorn trees.

Forestry

Forestry is important in the region and has a noticeable effect on the look of the landscape. The amount of deciduous woodland is slowly growing because as the mature coniferous plantations are being clearfelled, an increasing percentage are being replanted with broadleaf trees. In general terms, and although there are some areas of pine, most of the commercial coniferous forestry is dominated by spruce (mainly Sitka and Norway), and many of these plantations have matured and are being felled. Additionally, although larch woods were once common, due to the presence of Phytophthora disease, many of these plantations have been felled or are due to be felled in next few years. Natural Resources Wales are replanting all these felled

Sheep farm.

Forestry operations.

Clearfelling.

Coppiced woodland.

areas with a more diverse range of species in order to help combat the spread of any diseases in the future. As a result, many areas that were once smothered under serried ranks of conifers are now being returned to more open broadleaved woodland, and this is particularly true where the plantations were previously planted on ancient woodland sites. It is good to know that native species will figure more generally in future replanting.

Where patches of older deciduous woodland remain, almost all have seen some form of management, most usually in the form of coppicing. This involves cutting down most of the tree but leaving the stump, which then grows new shoots, thus producing a renewable crop of timber. Ancient hazel coppices can be found all around the region.

Roman road.

ARCHAEOLOGY

There are over 250 ancient monuments in the Brecon Beacons National Park, including hillforts, standing stones, stone circles, hut circles, chambered tombs and burial cairns. There is evidence that people have been here since the Mesolithic period at the end of the last Ice Age, roughly 12,000 years ago. Charcoal and artefacts found in upland peat bogs indicate that these early people were burning scrubland to create clearings where it would be easier to hunt grazing animals, and possibly to begin some form of basic agriculture. Later, during the Neolithic period (about 7,000 years ago), there was more widespread clearance of woodland to create space for crops and domestic animals, and this clearance continued into the Bronze Age (about 5,000 years ago) and accelerated into the Iron Age (about 3,000 years ago). The building of hillforts around this time suggests there may have been conflict over cleared land. Despite the fact that the clearances have continued ever since, the landscape we see today is little changed from how it would have been at the time of the Roman invasion. The main exceptions are the quarries of the industrial revolution, water-supply reservoirs, commercial forestry, and the expansion of towns and villages.

Several of the large 'beacon' cairns that dot the region have been here since the Bronze Age, and many of the standing stones and stone circles are even older. However, archaeology is not just about ancient times; it

Packhorse trail.

Stone circle on Mynydd Bach Trecastell.

Maen Llia – standing stone.

Crug Hywel – Iron Age hillfort.

Plane wreck on Fan Hir.

is also concerned with more recent events, and there is a wealth of archaeological heritage here, from ancient hillforts to more modern industrial workings, from prehistoric burial sites to medieval castles, and from stone circles to World War II plane wrecks. The people who called this landscape their home, who lived, worked and died here, have left behind physical traces that can tell us much about their lives. It is the diverse archaeology of the region that helps to make it such a special place.

Keep your eyes open, particularly when on the upland heaths, as new archaeological discoveries are being made here on a fairly regular basis. If you do spot something that you believe may be of archaeological interest, please do not disturb it or move any stones as you may, unwittingly, be destroying vital information of use to archaeologists. Unusual or suspicious finds should be reported to Cadw (see the 'Further Information' section at the back of the book).

Derelict mill.

INDUSTRY

Many visitors comment on how lucky I am to live in such an unspoilt area. My reaction sometimes confuses them. The fact is that nowhere in Britain has escaped the hand of man, and the land within the Brecon Beacons National Park is no exception. The area has been exploited since time immemorial for stone, and back in the early 19th century the southern borders were at the heart of industrial Wales. Although much of the industry has long since disappeared, there are still tantalising signs of it, even in the uplands. Of particular note are the limestone quarries and their associated lime kilns, tilestone quarries, and tramroads. The area along the southern boundary of the Park was once full of industry, not just iron and coal, but also silica mines and a variety of mills ... all of which are now long abandoned. Their legacy is an area which is very important in terms of industrial archaeology, as demonstrated by the fact that Blaenavon is a World Heritage site.

Abandoned millstone.

Blaenavon iron works.

Limestone quarries

Limestone was originally quarried for building stone from small 'public' quarries, some of which date back to Norman times. Quarrying became more extensive in the mid-17th century, when improvements in farming techniques brought about by the agricultural revolution increased the demand for lime, which was used as a soil improver. However, most of the large quarries we see today are here as a result of the industrial revolution, and particularly the iron industry, which consumed huge quantities of limestone as a flux in the iron smelting process. Many limestone quarries were connected to ironworks by tramroads (see below).

Limekilns

There are limekilns all over the southern areas of the Park. These come in all shapes and sizes, from tiny family-run operations to huge batteries of kilns. The basic process is to sandwich layers of limestone cobbles with layers of charcoal (or coal) and then set the whole lot alight. The heat drives carbon dioxide from the limestone (which is basically calcium carbonate), and what results is pure lime (calcium oxide). Although this was used initially for agricultural lime, huge increases in population during the industrial revolution resulted in a corresponding increase in the demand for lime by the construction industry.

Pant-y-rhiw Quarry.

Hendre Quarry.

Limekiln at Herbert's Quarry.

Limekiln on Trefil Mountain.

Tilestone quarry.

Tilestone quarries

See also 'Tilestones' on page 30. Tilestone quarries date back to medieval times and were very important to the economy of the region until the advent of the railways, which made it easier to transport thinner, lighter slate from North Wales – 'imports' which effectively killed the local tilestone industry. In addition to the thin tilestones, thicker strata were quarried for flagstones and work-tops, and the thickest slabs were used for building stone, often being dressed on site. Several of the quarries in the Black Mountains still have piles of dressed stone that were never removed. Due to the location of the strata within the Old Red Sandstone, many quarries were sited high on the hillside, and the quarried material was carried into the valleys on horse-drawn sleds. The vestiges of sled paths can often be seen descending gently across the slopes below the quarries; sometimes looking like a shelf across the hillside; sometimes resembling a shallow cutting.

Tramroad at Llangattock.

Tramroads

There are hundreds of miles of tramroad in the region, many of which offer easy walking into spectacular areas that would otherwise be difficult to access. Classic examples include the Llangattock Quarries Tramroad, which traverses the awesome escarpment to the south of Crickhowell, and the Brinore Tramroad, which runs from Talybont-on-Usk to the quarries at Trefil, on the other side of the mountain. These tramroads were not railways as we know them, but 'plateways' formed by lengths of angle-iron held together by 'spreader bars', along which travelled horse-drawn tram carts with iron-rimmed wooden wheels. Later versions had solid iron wheels.

Tramroad near Penwyllt.

Replica tram cart.

Central Beacons on a busy day.

Dirt bikes.

COUNTRYSIDE PRESSURES

The Brecon Beacons National Park attracted well over four million visitors in 2014 (the latest year for which figures are available), and this number has increased year on year since then. Most are day visitors travelling by car, and it is not unknown for there to be traffic chaos at popular car parks in the Waterfall Country and at Storey Arms / Pont a'r Daf on the main road (A470) between Brecon and Merthyr Tydfil. The problem is compounded by the fact that Pen y Fan is currently **the** place to visit – most likely because it's the highest mountain in southern Britain. There can be literally hundreds of cars in the Storey Arms area on a warm summer weekend (and at other times), and it is rare now to get the summit to yourself… even (some might say especially) at sunrise and sunset. The mountain appears to be a victim of its own success.

Throughout the area, increasing visitor numbers result not only in traffic and parking issues, but also footpath erosion, and bodies such as the National Park Authority and the National Trust have major, ongoing footpath repair and maintenance programs because the underlying geology is such that footpath erosion quickly becomes a serious problem if remedial work is not done. This erosion is intensified in several areas by illegal dirt bike and four-wheel drive activity.

Despite these pressures, tourism is of vital importance here because it brings much needed money into the local economy. However, it needs to be carefully managed if it is to be sustainable. On the plus side, it creates jobs for local people, boosts the local economy by over £200 million a year, helps preserve rural services like village shops and public transport, and increases the demand for local crafts. On the minus side, it results in traffic congestion and pollution. Many of the tourism-related jobs are seasonal with low pay and long hours, and increased demand for holiday homes and rental properties makes the housing stock too expensive for local people.

Visitors come mainly to enjoy the scenery and see the wildlife, which creates additional pressure to conserve habitats, but there is also the danger that by encouraging tourism we are destroying the very thing the visitors want to see. There is inevitably damage to the landscape, not only in terms of erosion, but also in terms of disturbance to wildlife and locals. For example, a gate negligently left open by a passing group can result in a hill farmer having to spend hours gathering stray sheep. Litter, too, is a common issue, and the proximity of the National Park to the densely populated industrial valleys of South Wales means that fly-tipping is an ever-present problem.

Dogs are a highly-contentious issue, and even the best-behaved dog can cause problems. Many sheep are spooked by just the sight of a strange dog, particularly if it is not on a lead, and a pregnant ewe, having been scared by a dog, may even abort her foetus. A frightened sheep will panic and can injure itself if it runs into a wall or fence or, worse, tries to run across a stream or through steep rocky terrain. If the injuries are such that they require veterinary attention, such is the current market price of lamb that it may not be cost effective to have the sheep treated ... in which case it will be destroyed.

When walking in this area, please take time to consider your actions and how they impact the local environment. Use public transport whenever possible, for it is only by using it that it will improve; and if you drive here, please keep your speed down on the country lanes and park considerately. Buy locally, for without you the local shops will struggle to survive – in any case, you will often be amazed by the quality of the service and the goods on offer, the friendliness of the welcome and the reasonable prices.

Central Beacons on a busy day.

Dirt bike scars.

Litter.

Fly tipping.

Crickhowell High Street.

Path maintenance.

Never drop litter (this includes cigarette ends and fruit skins, which can take years to decompose) and please don't feed the wildlife (it only encourages it to seek more – often on the roads). In fact, if you see any litter, do your bit for the environment – pick it up and dispose of it properly.

Take nothing but photographs …

Kill nothing but time …

Keep nothing but memories …

Leave nothing but goodwill …

Llyn y fan fach.

Macnamara's road.

MYTHS AND LEGENDS

Wales is a country full of myths and legends. The landscape stirs the imagination, and the tradition of fireside story-telling is very strong. Here are just a few of the stories about the Brecon Beacons.

The Lady of the Lake and the Physicians of Myddfai

Perhaps the most famous tale to come out of the Brecon Beacons, this legend tells how a young shepherd boy called Gwyn spied a beautiful maiden at Llyn y Fan Fach in the wild Carmarthen Fans. Over a period of several weeks, he gained her confidence and eventually asked her to marry him, at which point he discovered that she was of faerie birth. Her father was loath to give his consent, but he eventually relented and gave them a dowry of livestock. However, he also said that the shepherd should never hit her, for on the third 'causeless' blow his daughter would return to the lake along with her dowry. The couple set up home at Esgair Llaethdy where they raised three sons, the eldest of whom was named Rhiwallon. To cut a long story short, although the marriage was happy, the shepherd eventually struck the third 'causeless' blow, upon which his wife walked back to the lake where she disappeared along with all the livestock. It is said that Gwyn was so distraught that he plunged into the lake and drowned. Meanwhile, the sons spent weeks searching for their mother, who eventually appeared and told Rhiwallon that he and his descendants were destined to become the most skilful physicians in the country. She then led them to Pant y Meddygon (the Physicians' Dingle; just north of Usk Reservoir), where she taught them the art of herbal healing, telling them to record their knowledge in writing for the benefit of all mankind.

So much for legend. What is undisputed fact is that, in the early 13th century, a man named Rhiwallon Feddyg was the personal physician of Rhys Gryg, Lord of Dinefwr and the warrior son of the Welsh Prince, Rhys ap Gruffydd. Rhiwallon had three sons, Cadwgan, Gruffydd and Einion, and they and their descendants became famous for their skill as physicians, not just in Wales, but throughout Europe. Their medical wisdom is recorded in the Red Book of Hergest, a 14th-century manuscript currently kept in the Bodleian Library, which shows that the Physicians' healing powers were based on herbs, all of which grew locally around Pant y Meddygon, and many of which still thrive in the area. The last named 'Physician of Myddfai', John Jones, died in 1739, and his tombstone lies in the porch of St Michael's church in the village of Myddfai.

Macnamara's Road

Like so many stories, this tale is largely apocryphal, although it does have a strong factual foundation. What follows is merely a brief summary of one of several versions. Sir John Macnamara was squire of Llangoed Hall near Llyswen. Allegedly a founder member of the Hellfire Club and an inveterate gambler, he won the land in the Grwyne Fechan Valley in a poker game but promised the valley would be returned to its previous owner when he was 'no longer on the land'. As you will see, this wording is important. He built a house for his several mistresses in the woods at the end of the valley, and then built a road across the high mountain ridge so he could visit them more easily from Llyswen. The house (known as the Hermitage) and the road (Macnamara's Road) are both still in existence. One night, racing along his road to get to the Hermitage, he was thrown from his carriage and killed, whereupon the previous owner of the valley thought he would get his land back. However, despite the fact that this was the late

Mrs Macnamara's boundary stones.

18th century and women had few rights, Sir John's widow proved to be a formidable businesswoman! Far from selling up and moving away, she had a special mausoleum built in Llyswen so that Sir John's body was laid to rest 'on the land'! She also had boundary stones erected all around the edge of her land, basically telling the locals (who included the iron master, Sir Joseph Bailey) to keep their thieving hands off! A plucky lady.

Porth yr Ogof and the White Horse Pool

Way back in the mists of time, a beautiful princess lived in what is now known as the waterfall country and often rode through the Mellte Valley on a great, white stallion. One day she was set upon by a band of brigands and fearing for her life (and probably her modesty), she rode into the Mellte gorge and into Porth yr Ogof – a cave with a huge entrance. The Dark Ages were, of course, Arthurian times, and Merlin, sensing that something was afoot, picked up the princess's cry for help. Watching events unfold in his crystal ball, he realised that a successful outcome demanded instant action, so he ordered the river to rise up in flood and sweep away the brigands. Unfortunately, Merlin was not the most accomplished of wizards, and he failed to think his actions through to their logical conclusion. Yes, the brigands were all swept away and drowned – but the princess and her

The White Horse Pool.

white charger were also in the path of the flood! Merlin was so upset that his actions had caused the death of both the princess and her horse, that he caused their images to be forever graven on the rocks where they died. The horse drowned in the pool, and there is the image of a horse on the far wall of the entrance chamber; the princess drowned in a chamber deep inside the cave where there is a stalagmite that resembles a fair maiden.

Llyn Cwm Llwch: The Fairy Door and other such tales

Nestled at the head of the valley between Pen y Fan and Corn Du, the two highest peaks in the Central Beacons, lies Llyn Cwm Llwch, a tranquil pool trapped behind a wall of debris left behind when the ice and snow of the last ice age finally melted. A pool full of legends, it is supposed to be bottomless, and it is said that if all bell ropes from Llanfaes Church (in Brecon) were tied end-to-end, they would not reach the bottom. According to several sources, the entrance to Fairyland is by the shores of the lake, and this secret door was once opened by the Queen of the Fairies each May Day so that we, mere mortals, could visit her realm. Access was freely given until, one day, an ungracious visitor stole a flower from a fairy, and brought it back to the real world, since which time no mortal has been

Llyn Cwm Llwch.

able to find any sign of the fairy door. It is also said that, some years after the fairy door was closed, a group of people from Brecon decided to drain the lake in order to find the fairy treasure that was undoubtedly buried there. They cut a trench through the moraine dam, and as the water level began to drop, an island appeared in the middle of the lake, upon which appeared a bearded giant in a flowing white gown. He spoke to them (in Welsh) in a booming voice and told them in no uncertain terms to go away and leave him alone. "If anyone disturbs my peace again, I will cause the waters of the lake to rise up and flood the town of Brecon".

Tommy Jones

One of the most poignant tales is that of little Tommy Jones – a true story which has been elevated to legendary status. On August 4th 1900 William Jones, a miner from the Rhondda, decided to take his five-year-old son, Tommy, to visit his grandparents who farmed near Brecon. After a long and tiring journey they eventually arrived in Brecon at about 6pm, from where they started the 6km walk to Cwm Llwch Farm where Tommy's grandparents lived. Just before 8pm, they reached a tented army camp at a place called the Login where they stopped for a drink, and William bought Tommy a pennyworth of biscuits as a special treat. Tommy's grandfather strolled by as they were resting, accompanied by Tommy's cousin – 13-year-old Willie John. William had not yet finished his drink, so the two men sent Willie John to the farmhouse, less than 500 metres away, to warn of the imminent arrival of guests. Tommy decided to accompany him, so they ran off together along the well-defined track. Although they had to cross two rough plank bridges not far from the Login, the journey was not difficult, but it must have been quite frightening for a young boy whose home was in the back-to-back housing of an industrial valley. Twilight was falling, and farm animals seen along the way must have appeared like monsters from a fairy tale. The two boys had travelled less than half the distance to the farmhouse when Tommy started to cry and wanted to go back to his father. So, they parted. Willie John continued to the farm, and Tommy ran back towards the Login, less than 250 metres away. Having delivered his message, Willie John returned to the Login, arriving less than 10 minutes since they had parted; but there was no sign of Tommy. Immediately they learned what had happened, William and Tommy's grandfather set off along the track to search. Twenty minutes later, having returned to the Login, they were joined in their search by the soldiers, but even though it was impossible that Tommy could have travelled far, not a trace was found. The search that ensued went on for weeks and involved huge numbers of people including troops, police, farmers, local residents and other volunteers. The Daily Mail offered £20.00 (a princely sum in those days) to anyone who could solve the puzzle, the reward being announced in the paper, on posters, and by the Brecon Town Crier. After three weeks of intensive searching there was not even the slightest clue as to how little Tommy had so completely disappeared. Time passed.

Just under four weeks after the initial incident, Mrs Hamer, the wife of a gardener from Castle Madoc (a large house about 10km north of Brecon), started having a vivid, recurring dream. Although she had never visited the area, she dreamt she saw a high ridge running from a flat-topped mountain, and at a point directly above a small round lake she saw the body of a young boy. She described her dream to her husband, who recognised the scene

The Tommy Jones obelisk (and right).

THIS OBELISK
MARKS THE SPOT
WHERE THE BODY OF
TOMMY JONES
AGED 5 WAS FOUND
HE LOST HIS WAY
BETWEEN CWMLLWCH
FARM AND THE LOGIN
ON THE NIGHT OF
AUGUST 4TH 1900
AFTER AN ANXIOUS SEARCH
OF 29 DAYS HIS REMAINS
WERE DISCOVERED SEPT 2ND
ERECTED BY VOLUNTARY
SUBSCRIPTIONS
W POWELL PRICE
MAYOR OF BRECON 1901

as he had visited the Beacons several times, and on Sunday, September 2nd, she persuaded him to take her and some relatives to the area. They walked past Cwm Llwch Farm, up to Llyn Cwm Llwch, and then scrambled steeply up onto the ridge, aiming for a spot chosen by Mrs Hamer. There, to their horror, they found the remains of a small body. It was carried down and identified later that day as being Tommy. At the inquest, which was held on the following Tuesday, there was a unanimous verdict of 'death by exhaustion and exposure'. However no one could explain how 5-year-old Tommy, having already had a long and tiring day, had reached a point 685 metres above sea level, almost 400 metres above the Login and more than three kilometres distant (as the crow flies) across extremely difficult terrain, in the dark. The mystery remains.

Pwll Gwy-rhoc – the Witches' Pool

In the middle of Mynydd Llangatwg (Llangattock Mountain) lies a dark and foreboding lake known locally as the Witches' Pool. There seems to be no reason for its existence as the land slopes away from it in at least two directions. It is said that it lies at the centre of a bloody battle that was fought here in the Dark Ages, and that due to the amount of blood and gore the vegetation never had a chance to recover before it slowly sank below the level of the moor. The area has an eerie, almost malevolent atmosphere, and the water looks as if it's full of dried blood. If you stand on the shore and look at the near horizon through 360°, every high point

The Witches' Pool.

has (or had) a burial cairn on it! The stuff of legend, perhaps, but it's now accepted in scholarly circles that a great battle was fought here in 728AD, between Ethelbald the Mercian and the men of Morgannwg led by Rhodri Molwynog. The Mercians were heavily defeated in what ancient manuscripts describe as a blood bath. There is seldom smoke without fire!

The Skirrid *(Ysgyryd Fawr)*: the Holy Mountain

The Skirrid is a fine hill overlooking Abergavenny, at the eastern end of the Beacons Way. There is a noticeable ravine at its north-western end – the result of a post-glacial landslip (see page 50) – and there are many legends associated with the reason. It is said that the ravine was caused by the keel of Noah's Ark brushing against the hillside as the Great Flood receded, and that the landslide occurred at the moment of Christ's crucifixion. There is a strange, almost ominous-looking rock called the 'Devil's Pulpit' perched above the ravine, and legend has it that the Devil called local folk to this point and preached to them from the pulpit, telling them to bow down and worship him. The God-fearing locals naturally gave him short shrift, and he was so annoyed that he caused the land to shake – thus causing the landslip! Legend aside, the tiny St Michael's Chapel once stood on the summit, where Catholics celebrated mass during the Reformation. The bases of the two stone door posts are all that remain.

The Skirrid.

The Devil's Pulpit.

Winter ice in the Black Mountains.

Waterfall country.

LAST THOUGHTS

Welsh place names

Place names in Wales are often very descriptive, so a little knowledge of Welsh can literally bring the landscape to life.

Aber = river mouth, sometimes confluence

Aderyn = bird

Afon = river

Agen = cleft, fissure, cave

Allt / Gallt = hill, slope, wooded slope

Allwedd = key

Arian = silver, silvery

Arosfa = sheepwalk, a place to pause or stop, a layby

Bach = little, small

Ban / y Fan, pl. Bannau = peak, mountain, bare hill, beacon

Banc = bank, hillock, breast of a hill

Bedd, pl. Beddau = grave, tomb

Bedwen, pl. Bedw = birch

Berllan [mutation, see Perllan] = orchard

Betws = chapel of rest / small house of prayer [Arch.]

Blaen, pl. Blaenau = end, head, source of river, upland

Bod = dwelling, church

Bont [mutation, see Pont] = bridge

Braich = arm, headland, ridge, creek

Brith = speckled

Bro = region, land, one's square mile

Bron = breast of hill

Bryn = hill

Bugail, pl. Bugeiliaid = shepherd, herdsman

Bwlch = pass, col, gap

Bychan = small

Cadair = chair, chair shaped mound or hill, fort

Cadno = fox

Cae, pl. Caeau = field, enclosed land

Caer, pl. Caerau = fort

Calch = lime, chalk

Cam = crooked

Canol = middle

Capel = chapel

Carn, Carnedd = cairn, tumulus

Carreg, pl. Cerrig = rock, stone

Castell = castle, prominent rock

Cefn = ridge

Celli, Y Gelli = grove

Celynen, pl. celyn = holly

Cemais, Cemaes = river bend

Ceunant = ravine

Cil, pl. Ciliau = corner or angle, nook

Cilfach, y Gilfach = nook

Clawdd = earth bank, hedge, ditch

Clog, pl. Clogau = cliff

Clun = meadow, moor

Clydach = torrent, place near a river

Coch = red

Coed = woodland, trees

Collen = hazel

Comin = common

Corlan = sheepfold, pen

Corn = horn, mountain top

Cornel = corner

Cors = bog

Craig, y Graig, pl. Creigiau = cliff, rock

Crib, y Grib = crest

Croes, y Groes = cross, cross-roads

Crug, pl. Crugiau = hillock, cairn

Cwar = quarry

Cwm = deep narrow valley, valley

Cwrt = yard, court, grange

Cylch, pl. Cylchau = circle, surroundings

Cymer, pl. Cymerau = confluence

Dan = under, below

Derwen, pl. Derw or Deri = oak

Darren [mutation, see Tarren] = precipice, rocky hill, poor land

Dau = two

Dôl, pl. Dolydd, Dolau = meadow

Dinas = fort, settlement

Diserth = hermitage, retreat

Draw = yonder

Dre, Dref [mutation, see Tref] = Hamlet, town

Du = black, shaded

Dulais = dark stream [only as a river name]

Dwfr, Dŵr= water

Dwy = two (feminine form of Dau)

Dyffryn = valley

Eglwys = church

Eira = snow

Eithin = gorse

Eos = nightingale

Esgair = long ridge

Fach [mutation, see Bach] = small

Fan [mutation, see Ban] = peak

Fawr [mutation, see Mawr] = large

Fechan = little [only when mutated and feminine form of Bychan]

Felin [mutation, see Melin] = mill

Ffald, pl. Ffaldau = sheepfold, farmyard

Ffawydden, pl. ffawydd = beech

Ffin = boundary, border

Ffordd = road

Ffos = ditch, gutter

Ffridd = mountain pasture, moorland

Ffrwd, pl. Ffrydiau = (swift flowing) stream, torrent

Ffynnon, pl. Ffynhonnau = spring, well

Foel [mutation, see Moel] = a bare hill, summit

Fron [mutation, see Bron] = hillside

Gadair / Gader [see Cadair] = chair

Gallt = [mutation, see Allt] hillside

Gardd, pl. Gerddi = garden

Garth = enclosure, hill

Garw = rough

Glan = river bank, shore, slope

Glas = green, blue

Gleisiad = young salmon

Gleision = whey or adj. blue

Glyn = glen, valley

Goch = [mutation, see Coch] red

Gors = [mutation, see Cors] bog, marsh

Gwaun, pl. Gweunydd = moor

Gwen (f) = white

Gwern = alder, marsh

Gwlad = country

Gwrach = witch

Gwylfa = viewpoint [Disgwylfa means place to wait]

Gwyllt = wild

Gwyn = [mutation, see wyn, wen] white

Gwynt = wind

Gwyntog = windy

Gwyrlod, Gweirglodd = meadow

Hafod, Hafoty, Lluest = summer dwelling

Helygen, pl. helyg = willow

Hen = old

Hendre = winter dwelling

Heol, hewl = road

Hir, pl. hirion = long

Isaf, isha = lower

Llan = enclosure, church, parish

Llannerch = clearing, glade

Llech, pl. llechau = stone, slab

Llethr = slope

Llety = lodging

Llwch, pl. llychau = inlet, lake, marsh

Llwch eira = snow drift

Llwyd = grey

Llwyn = grove

Llyn, pl. llynnau = lake

Llys = hall or court

Llysiau = herbs, vegetables

Maen, y Faen, pl. meini = large stone, standing stone

Maenol, maenor = manor

Maerdy = dairy farm or demesne farm (attached to a manor house) or a steward's house in the Middle Ages

Maes, pl. meysydd = large open field

Mawn = peat

Mawr / Fawr = big, large

Melin / Y Felin = mill

Melindre = mill hamlet

Melyn = yellow

Merthyr = church consecrated by saint's bones, shrine

Mochyn, pl. moch = pig

Moel = bare hill, summit

Mynach = monk

Mynydd, pl. mynyddoedd = mountain

Nant, pl. nentydd = stream, valley

Neuadd = hall

Newydd = new

Odyn = kiln

Oer = cold

Ogof, pl. ogofau = cave

Onnen, pl. Ynn= ash tree

Pandy = fulling mill

Pant = hollow

Parc = park (high walled)

Pedair (f), pedwar (m) = four

Pen = top

Pennant = valley head [lit. stream head]

Pentre = village

Perfedd = middle

Perllan = orchard

Pigwrn = pinnacle

Pistyll = spring or spout

Plas = manor house

Pont = bridge

Porth = gateway also port

Pren = wooden

Pwll = pool, pit

Rhaeadr = waterfall

Rhedyn = bracken

Rhiw = hill

Rhos, pl. Rhosydd = moorland

Rhyd = ford

Sain, san, sant = saint

Sarn, pl. sarnau = old road

Sticil or camfa = stile

Sych = dry

Tafarn, pl. tafarnau = inn

Tair (f) Tri (m) = three

Tal = end

Tan = below

Tarren = rocky hill or knoll

Teg = fair

Tir = land

Tomen = mound

Traeth = beach

Trallwng = wet or muddy pool

Traws = across

Tre, tref = settlement or town

Tri (m) Tair (f) = three

Troed = foot

Trum, pl. trumau = ridge, peak

Twrch = boar

Twyn = hillock

Tŷ, pl. tai = house

Tyddyn = cottage or freeholding

Tyle = slope

Tywarchen = turf

Uchaf = upper

Uchel = high

Un = one

Waun [mutation, see Gwaun] = moor

Wen, wyn [mutation, see Gwen, Gwyn] = white

Y Wern [mutation, see Gwern] = swamp, alder,

Y Wrach [mutation, see Gwrach] = witch

Y, yr, `r = the

Ychen, pl. ych = ox

Yn = in

Ynys = island

Ysgol = school

Ystrad = valley floor

Further information

Below are listed some of the books I used in my research. A few are out of print, but copies are often available online or in second-hand book shops. I made extensive use of several of the excellent Collins Nature Guides to Britain and Europe, including *Wild Flowers*, *Herbs & Healing Plants*, *Mushrooms & Toadstools*, *Trees*, *Insects*, *Birds*, and *Butterflies & Moths*.

Brecon Beacons, Jonathan Mullard. Collins New Naturalist Library, 2014.

Complete Guide to British Insects, Michael Chinery. Collins, 2009.

Culpeper's Colour Herbal, Nicholas Culpeper. Arcturus Publishing, 2009.

Dictionary of the Place-Names of Wales. Hywel Wyn Owen a Richard Morgan. Gomer, 2007

Encyclopedia of Wild Flowers, John Akeroyd. Dempsey Parr, 1999.

Fascinated by Fungi, Pat O'Reilly. First Nature, 2016.

Ferns, Mosses & Lichens of Britain and Northern & Central Europe, Hans Martin Jahns. Collins, 1983.

Llyfr Adar Iolo Williams – Cymru ac Ewrop, addasiad Peter Hayman a Rob Hume. Gwasg Carreg Gwalch, 2004.

Llyfr Natur Iolo, addasiad Iolo Williams a Bethan Wyn Jones. Gwasg Carreg Gwalch, 2007.

Myths & Legends of the Brecon Beacons, Horatio Clare. Graffeg, 2017.

Nature of Snowdonia, Mike Raine. Pesda Press, 2010.

The Birds of Britain & Europe, Hermann Heinzel, R. S. R. Fitter, & John Parslow. Collins, 1979.

The Hedgerow Handbook, Adele Nozedar. Square Peg, 2012.

Welsh Legends and Myths, Graham Watkins. Lulu, 2018.

Wild Flowers of Britain and Northern Europe, Richard Fitter, Alastair Fitter, & Marjorie Blamey. Collins, 1996.

Useful websites

I made extensive use of the internet. Here are a few of the many sites I found useful.

www.bats.org.uk – The Bat Conservation Trust is the leading NGO solely devoted to the conservation of bats and the landscapes on which they rely.

www.beacons-npa.gov.uk – The official site of the Brecon Beacons National Park.

www.botanicalkeys.co.uk – A good plant identification site.

www.breconbeacons.org – The visitor portal of the Brecon Beacons National Park.

www.breconbeaconsbirder.com – Some brilliant images of birds and animals.

www.britishlichensociety.org.uk and wales-lichens.org.uk – Two sites giving information about lichens.

www.cadw.gov.wales – Cadw is the Welsh Government's historic environment service working for an accessible and well-protected historic environment in Wales.

www.first-nature.com – A great site with lots of information about a wide range of flora and fauna.

www.fforestfawrgeopark.org.uk – The website of the Fforest Fawr Geopark.

www.pfaf.org – A fascinating website giving edible, medicinal and other uses of over 7,000 plants.

www.rspb.org.uk – All you ever wanted to know about birds.

www.ukmoths.org.uk – All you ever wanted to know about moths.

www.uksafari.com – A general wildlife site with lots of information.

www.welshwildlife.org – Lots of information about wildlife from the Wildlife Trust of South & West Wales.

wildflowerfinder.org.uk – A great source of information about plants.

INDEX